IMAGES
of *America*

SOUTH NORWOOD

IMAGES
of America

SOUTH NORWOOD

South Norwood Committee
and the Norwood Historical Society

ARCADIA
PUBLISHING

Published by Arcadia Publishing
Charleston, South Carolina

Library of Congress Catalog Card Number: 2004108183

For all general information contact Arcadia Publishing at:
Telephone 843-853-2070
Fax 843-853-0044
E-mail sales@arcadiapublishing.com
For customer service and orders:
Toll-Free 1-888-313-2665

Visit us on the Internet at www.arcadiapublishing.com

CONTENTS

ACKNOWLEDGMENTS

The past quarter-century has seen small towns with their own unique identities become densely populated, homogenized suburbs. Meanwhile, family-run businesses and stores have given way first to regional chains and then to huge, warehouse-sized enterprises. Yet, while we mourn the loss of local businesses, personal service, and the simpler lifestyle they have come to symbolize, South Norwood reminds us that it is through neighbors working together that a community is built.

While not a comprehensive history, this compilation explores the experience of the residents of South Norwood over more than a century. Despite differences in language, religion, and culture, the early immigrants worked together to build a community, make a living, and raise their children. The neighborhood continues to be richly diversified, with new immigrants joining families that have been here for generations. In the photographs and captions that follow, we hope to capture some of the spirit and distinctiveness of the neighborhood— characteristics that still exist today.

We would like to extend our appreciation to the following individuals and organizations who loaned their photographs, shared their stories, and helped us compile this history of South Norwood: Brenda Babel, Stephanie Babel, Josephine Bader, Helen Balen, Patty Bailey, Janina Benkavitch, Lillian Bielski, Cindy Buscone, Mike Cawley, Francesca and Henry Cergueira, Mark Chubet, Alice Cofsky, John Correia, Frank DaCosta, Angela Daly, Christina DaSilva, Dale Day, Donna DiMarzo, Bob Donahue, Helen Abdallah Donohue, Dolores Elias, Florence Esper, Joseph Eysie, Paul Eysie, Ellie Gallant, Irene Gotovich, Bob Hansen, Fred Howard, Philip Howard, Aira Koski Johnson, Sean Keegan, Rev. Joseph Kimmett, Edward Kniolek, George Kornak, Ed Kwiatkowski, Tom Lambert, Henry Maddocks, Lillian Martowska, Betty Ann McCarthy, Rich McCarthy, Donald McLean, Michael and Samera Mike, Gerry Miller, Ted Mulvehill, Cheryl Nardelli, Ernie Paciorkowski, Frank and Bill Phipps, Michael Quinn, Marion Redonnet, Alfredo and Margarida Rodrigues, Mario and Maria Rodrigues, George Saad, Jackie Howard Saber, Anne Sansone, Peter Santoro, Frani Sarantos, Dave Silva, Antionette Troilo, Tony Troilo, Michael and Lena Triventi, Kenneth and Janet Webber, Rev. William Wolkovich, Balch Elementary School, Morrill Memorial Library, Morse House Restoration Committee, Norwood Historical Society, Norwood Recreation Department, Rancho Folclorico do Alto Minho, South Norwood Committee, St. George's Orthodox Church, and St. George's Roman Catholic Church.

—Patricia J. Fanning and Heather S. Cole

INTRODUCTION

The decades before and after the turn of the 20th century were the most intensive periods of immigration in United States history. In the 40 years from 1860 to 1900, 14 million immigrants arrived in America, while the single decade from 1901 to 1910 brought almost 9 million. More significantly, more than 70% of these new immigrants were natives of Southern and Eastern Europe who were fleeing political turmoil. They were predominantly young, rural, poor, unskilled, and uneducated. These young immigrants were quickly drawn to cities and industrial communities where they could obtain employment as laborers and create a refuge from the often disdainful American mainstream. This book explores the history and evolution of one such immigrant enclave: South Norwood, Massachusetts.

Norwood gained its independence from the town of Dedham in 1872. At its inception, Norwood was a fairly homogeneous community of Yankee stock anchored by the Congregational church. During the next half-century, however, existing factories expanded and new enterprises arrived, making Norwood an important industrial center that attracted a substantial number of immigrant laborers. This, in itself, was not new. Earlier in the 19th century, the town had absorbed Irish and German workers, who had gathered in neighborhoods informally identified as Dublin, Cork City, and Germantown. Although these inhabitants faced some discrimination upon their arrival, a limited amount of prosperity had brought them stability and respectability.

By 1910, however, the population of Norwood had nearly quadrupled, with foreign-born residents comprising an ever-increasing percentage. The more-recent arrivals were from Eastern Europe and Scandinavia, and they resided primarily in the heretofore sparsely populated southern end of town. Geographically, South Norwood was roughly triangular, bordered on two sides by the tracks of the New York, New Haven, & Hartford Railroad, and it was a considerable distance from the commercial center of town. Inexpensive, multifamily dwellings were quickly erected, but they could not keep up with the surging influx of immigrants. For decades, the South Norwood neighborhood—nicknamed "The Flats"—was viewed as if it were foreign territory. According to a 1916 local newspaper account, "A great number of people have never visited this section of town," which gives an indication both of how rapidly the neighborhood had developed, and how marginalized its residents were. A later historian, Bryant Tolles, concluded that the district "long remained a shabby, unsanitary, and poorly provided place to live," an area where "the new foreigners had literally been herded together practically as outcasts."

Within South Norwood itself, however, the reality was more complex. As chain migrations from Lithuania, Poland, Syria, Italy, and Portugal continued, a vital, ethnically diverse commercial district sprang up to meet the needs of the neighborhood's inhabitants. Small businesses and stores of all types, including many multilingual establishments, lined the main street. There were tailors, barbers, grocers, bakeries, fruit markets, meat markets, photographic studios, ethnic co-operatives, restaurants, and laundries in almost every available storefront. Lithuanian and Polish families built two Catholic churches: St. George's in 1915 and St. Peter's in 1920. The Syrian population erected St. George's Orthodox Church shortly thereafter. Charitable associations and social clubs provided support and a wide range of activities. The neighborhood flourished.

The heavily populated side streets of South Norwood were characterized by modest triple-decker houses, expansive gardens on small plots, and an international ambiance. A cooperative spirit dominated the area as immigrants joined together to make the most of life in America. They learned enough of each other's languages and customs to communicate, and after working long hours at nearby factories, husbands and wives found time to make new friends.

The Balch School, located in the center of the neighborhood, became South Norwood's heart and soul. Not only did the multiethnic community of children receive their education there, but countless adults attended English and Americanization classes at the school as well. As the decades passed, people started more businesses, purchased their homes, made improvements to their properties, and educated their sons and daughters. Though still viewed with suspicion and disdain by many in American society, the immigrants embraced their new country and sent their children off to war. Those who were lost in the war were mourned and commemorated; those who returned were celebrated. This younger generation, more often than not, remained in the neighborhood where they were raised.

The post–World War II era caused many communities across the country to undergo significant change. Privately owned businesses and industrial entrepreneurs gave way to corporate conglomerates, while the blue-collar work force declined. Towns like Norwood that had once been nearly self-contained communities where people lived, worked, and shopped, were transformed into residential-industrial suburbs, virtual bedroom communities providing housing for bureaucratic employees. These changes hit South Norwood particularly hard, as many of the large factories closed their doors or moved out of town, leaving residents unemployed or with small pensions. Local businesses lost their clientele to shopping centers, plazas, and mammoth shopping malls. The loss of both Catholic parishes, St. Peter's in 1997 and St. George's in 2004, saddened longtime residents.

Today, South Norwood is on the rebound. Storefronts, restaurants, and businesses are returning, and the neighborhood remains remarkably stable. Its residents are often third-generation inhabitants, people who can point out the window to the homes of aunts, uncles, grandparents, and lifelong friends.

The risks, struggles, and triumphs of the generations who have made South Norwood a unique "community within a community" deserve to be documented and remembered. The story is told here through the photographs, recollections, and generosity of the people themselves. They remain proud of their multicultural heritage, and confident in the future of their distinctively American neighborhood.

One

CREATING A COMMUNITY

This c. 1885 photograph shows South Norwood just prior to the influx of immigrants who would transform this bucolic scene into a vibrant, multicultural community. By the turn of the 20th century, these railroad tracks were bringing Lithuanian, Polish, Syrian, Italian, and Portuguese immigrants to work in local factories and mills. Within 25 years, Washington Street (seen in the left background) was lined with ethnic markets, cooperatives, and triple-decker houses.

One of the first ethnic groups to settle in South Norwood were Lithuanians. Vincas "Vincent" Kudirka left his home village of Ziliai in western Lithuania to avoid military conscription, and arrived in Norwood in 1902. Kudirka eventually found work at the Winslow Brothers & Smith tannery, where he met Anastasia Venskus. The two were married in May 1910 and raised three children.

Two distinct groups of Lithuanian immigrants settled in South Norwood. One, a group of secular, leftist-leaning citizens, built Lithuanian Hall on St. George Avenue in 1914. The other, a group of Roman Catholics, built the first church in South Norwood, St. George's, in 1915. The church founders shown in this 1937 photograph are, from left to right, as follows: (first row) Andrius Saulenas, Karolius Klimavicius, Rev. Stephen Kneizis, Vincas Kudirka, and Kastantas Akstinas; (second row) Pranas Kuras, Jonas Ruskys, Pranas Kudirka, and Ignas Grudinskas.

Frances Busaite and Maciei "Michael"
Smolski were among the early Lithuanian
immigrants and original planners
of St. George's Roman Catholic
Church in South Norwood. They
were married c. 1910 and lived in a
two-family home on Folan Avenue.

Polish immigrants constituted another early group that settled in South Norwood. Sophie
Gotoveckhi and Stanley Matusewicz, both raised in Vilna, Poland, did not meet until they
had immigrated to Boston. Sophie and Stanley, seated at center, were married in June 1919,
then relocated to South Norwood, where they both worked at the Winslow Brothers & Smith
tannery, and raised eight children. When their children entered school, their surname was
Americanized to Martowska.

Although many immigrants found work in local factories, there existed a number of entrepreneurs among the new settlers. Konstanty "Connie" Jankowski was 16 years old when he left Krakow, Poland. He met fellow émigré Mary Stravenski in the United States. The two married in 1917 and settled on Weld Avenue in South Norwood, where they raised three daughters. From 1925 to 1944, Connie owned Crystal Market at 1182 Washington Street.

Joseph G. Howard was one of the first Syrian settlers in South Norwood. By 1900, after living in Boston for a time, Howard had bought land at the intersection of today's Washington and Cedar Streets, and was working in the Bird & Son paper mill in East Walpole. Later, he opened a grocery store on Washington Street. Howard was one of the founders of St. George's Orthodox Church in 1921.

Syrian immigrant Habib Tomm owned a handkerchief factory in Boston in the 1890s. He and his wife, Damlah, moved to South Norwood *c.* 1902 and opened a factory on Dean Street. Their Boston employees traveled to Norwood by train to work in the factory.

John Boo Abdallah emigrated from Syria with his wife, Fasouh Hanna, and son Nicholas. They settled in Boston, and opened a dry goods store on Kneeland Street. By 1911, the Abdallahs had relocated to South Norwood, where they opened South End Hardware, which is still a family-owned business. The Abdallahs were among the founders of St. George's Orthodox Church. Here, John sits in front of the family store *c.* 1940.

Located far from the commercial center of town and bordered by railroad tracks, South Norwood became a physically—as well as culturally—distinct neighborhood. In 1897, after a state recommendation that railroad bridges or underpasses be built to reduce fatal pedestrian accidents, this underpass was constructed. Known as Subway Hill, the new road redirected Washington Street under the railroad tracks and became the gateway to South Norwood.

Attracted by various industries, foreign-born workers began to pour into South Norwood at the turn of the 20th century. In response, real-estate developers quickly erected multifamily dwellings to house the immigrants. Primarily freestanding triple-deckers that comprised 3 to 12 apartments, these structures became a unique architectural feature of South Norwood. Between 1913 and 1917, more than 400 triple-deckers were built.

The origin of South Norwood's nickname, "The Flats," has always been unclear. Some say that the area itself, once farmland, was lower and "flatter" than the rest of town. Others state that the term was derived from the flat roofs of the triple-deckers that inhabited the area. Finally, in a modification of this story, still others believe the name came from the term identifying the apartments themselves, which were called "flats." The 1915 Sanborn Fire Insurance map lends some credence to the last explanation. On that map, a small portion of which is shown here, each existing structure was identified by its use or purpose, not by any architectural feature. For example, "fruit," "cobbler," and "tailor" are noted. Therefore, one may conclude that the multifamily dwellings located throughout South Norwood are identified as "flats" most likely because they contained apartments or "flats," not because of their roof construction.

Italian immigrants began arriving to South Norwood in the years between 1915 and 1925. Santo and Sarah (Colesta) D'Amico already had family in town when they left Abruzza, Italy, and traveled to South Norwood, where they first lived in a triple-decker at the intersection of Dean and Washington Streets. In this December 1964 photograph, the D'Amicos celebrate the return of their grandson David from basic training with the National Guard.

Dominick Triventi, seen here with his wife, Josephine, was 13 when he left Italy. He was drawn to South Norwood by a boyhood friend who spoke of the employment possibilities in the area. A charter member of the benefit society known as the Italian American Lodge No. 1235, Order Sons of Italy in America, Triventi was presented with the lodge's Man of the Century plaque in 1973.

16

Nick and Rose Troilo were seasick during most of their journey from Abruzza, Italy, to the port of Boston, according to stories they later told their children. When they left Italy, the pair were newly married and had not yet begun their family. Rose's brother Charlie had already immigrated to the United States, and may have sent word encouraging the Troilos to join him in South Norwood. Such chain migrations were common among families. The couple made their way to the neighborhood, where Nick found work at Bird & Son and his wife set about making a home on Talbot Avenue.

Many Portuguese immigrants were married men who left their families behind and came to the United States to work. Antonio Louis Rodrigues left a wife and son in Portugal when he came to South Norwood c. 1925. He sent money back home and visited every few years. His wife remained there, managing the family farm and raising their children. Antonio eventually rejoined her in Portugal after nearly 50 solitary years in South Norwood.

Other Portuguese immigrants married and started families in the United States. Joe Portas left the village of Paredes do Val c. 1925, and made his way to South Norwood, where he took a job in the American Brake Shoe & Foundry Company. He met and married his wife, Angelina, in Fall River and brought her back to South Norwood. The couple were photographed after their wedding, c. 1936.

18

Mario Rodrigues was born in Paredes do Val, Portugal, in 1938. Many of the men of his village worked abroad, and only visited home every few years. When Rodrigues was 12, he joined his father, Antonio Louis Rodrigues, in South Norwood. Mario returned to Portugal in 1963 to marry, and then brought his bride here. This image shows Mario and Maria Rodrigues shortly after their wedding.

Portuguese immigrants who came to the United States in later years were more likely to remain in this country. Silvester DaSilva Jr. was 25 years old when he joined his parents, who had immigrated here a few years prior. He returned to Portugal to marry Lucinda Vincente, and in 1972, the newlyweds made their home on Washington Street in South Norwood. Seen here are, from left to right, Silvester DaSilva Jr., wife Lucinda, and Silvester's parents, Maria and Silvester DaSilva Sr., in a photograph taken during a family vacation c. 1976.

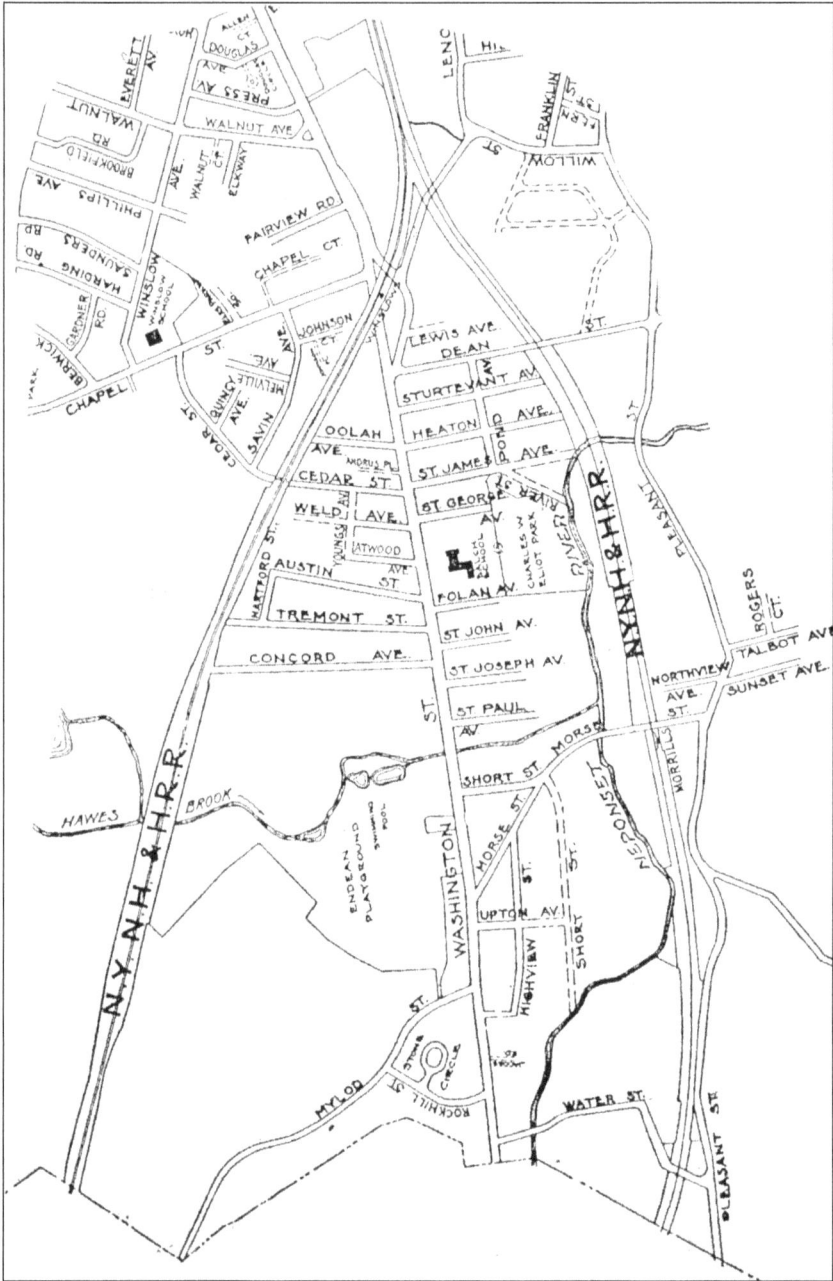

Immigrants who created a community from the open space that was the southernmost part of Norwood came from all over the world. As can be seen in this mid–20th century map, the neighborhood was bounded on two sides by railroad tracks and on the third by the border with the town of Walpole. Isolated geographically and culturally from the more established Norwood community, South Norwood's diverse population blossomed and created a self-contained habitat. Those who lived here recall a neighborhood of working-class families who respected one another and embraced difference. "We were all in the same boat," recollected one resident, "and we made the most of it. None of us had much, but in another sense, we were rich. There was such cooperation and kindness."

Two

THE FAITHS OF
OUR FATHERS

Churches played an important role in the development of South Norwood. Not all immigrants were religious, but those who were found their church communities to be a source of social activity and support during difficult times. In return, many immigrants dedicated numerous hours to teaching Sunday school, organizing church events, and raising funds for building and renovating church properties.

Lithuanians were the first ethnic group to establish a house of worship in South Norwood: St. George's Roman Catholic Church. Initially, the faithful had traveled to worship at a Lithuanian parish in South Boston. But in 1910, local Lithuanians decided to establish a mutual benefit society to provide for members in case of illness or death, and to satisfy members' spiritual needs as well.

In March 1912, members of the Lithuanian Benefit Society of St. George began raising money to buy a parcel of land on Baker Avenue (now St. James Avenue). After the members purchased the land, the construction of St. George's Roman Catholic Church began in the spring of 1915. The interior of the church is seen here.

As construction of St. George's Roman Catholic Church was nearing completion in the fall of 1915, the Reverend A. Daugis asked the cardinal of the Boston Archdiocese to formally bless the church, an event generally involving some ceremony and celebration. The cardinal at first declined, but upon further petition from members of the parish, he conceded. The Lithuanian community celebrated the long-awaited dedication of St. George's in September 1916. Members of Lithuanian and Catholic societies (pictured above and below), visiting clergy, local residents, and no less than six bands marched through town after the ceremony, waving American flags and banners. As many as 5,000 people attended the day's events, which culminated in sports, games, and an evening picnic at Dean Field.

Rev. Stephen Kneizis was the fourth pastor of St. George's, serving from 1931 to 1947. Born in Lithuania in 1897, Kneizis immigrated to the United States with his parents in 1914. A writer and translator as well as a pastor, he translated songs and hymns for his parishioners and plays for church youth groups. Held in high esteem by the archdiocese's Cardinal O'Connell, the Reverend Kneizis, like his predecessors, also offered Mass in Lithuanian.

Here, in 1937, Rev. Stephen Kneizis poses with parish alter boys in front of St. George's. A diligent and well-loved pastor, Kneizis was feted by his parishioners in 1947, on the 20th anniversary of his priesthood. Two days later, the priest died suddenly in his sleep. Not yet 50, he was greatly mourned by all in the parish.

Just as the men of St. George's organized into mutual benefit and fraternal societies, so did the women of the church take an active role in serving the spiritual needs of the community. In 1913, two years before the church was built, a prayer group and choir were organized, and meetings were held at homes in the community. Later, there would also be the Women's Alliance and a Single Ladies Sodality.

In the early 1950s, under the leadership of Rev. Felix Norbut, members of St. George's undertook fund-raising for a church convent, which was dedicated in September 1955. Parish demographics shifted, however, and by 1985, there were not enough children in the parish to sustain the convent in the role of educating young people. Since that time, the convent has been leased to sisters from various orders who serve several apostolates in the archdiocese.

For the first few years, local Polish immigrants attended Mass at St. George's Roman Catholic Church. But simmering ethnic tensions led the Polish community to desire a parish of its own, where services would be offered in the native language. In 1919, Polish Catholics met at the Southern Theatre on Washington Street to discuss establishing a second South Norwood church. The group acquired an old building on St. Joseph Avenue and converted it into a church. On Easter Sunday 1920, the first Mass was celebrated at St. Peter's Roman Catholic Church (above). The founders of St. Peter's included Rev. Alex Syski of Hyde Park, and South Norwood residents Joseph Adamonis, Anthony Jankowski, Constantine Jankowski, Michael Rusiecki, John Usewicz, and Constantine Walukiewicz. The interior of the small church is seen below.

Boleslaw "Billy" and Jadwiga Paciorkowski,
pictured at their 1912 wedding, were among
the early members of St. Peter's. Although
they lived closer to St. Catherine's Roman
Catholic Church, the couple attended St.
Peter's, traveling by horse-and-carriage
from their Neponset Street home to the
South Norwood church every Sunday.

The Reverend Cheshinski (seated fourth from left) poses with members of the St. Peter's Choir
c. 1927. Some of the members identified in this photograph are Mary Simaski, Ann Usevich,
Mary Laski, Antoinette Gotovich, Stacia Mackarevitch, Stanley Benkavitch, Walter Gotovich,
Boley Stanovich, and Mikey Simaski.

Rev. Hippolite J. Zawalich became pastor of St. Peter's in 1934. During his 21-year tenure, the church was remodeled inside and out, and the first church rectory was built next door. The rectory was dedicated in 1936.

Rev. Ferdinand V. Miszkin, pastor of St. Peter's from 1955 to 1971, also undertook extensive work to renovate the church. With the assistance of parishioners, the church was re-sided, the steeple rebuilt, and the interior refurbished to include an altar imported from Italy. The Reverend Miszkin's hobby was woodworking, and he personally built the side altars, confessionals, and the cross that sat atop the steeple.

On a beautiful May day in 1946, Edmund Gromelski and Veronica Zabrowski were united in marriage at St. Peter's. Seen here are the couple's attendants, who were photographed as they exited the church. From left to right (front to back) are the following: Helen Radzwill and Tony Alex; Olga Olsavitch and Al Simmons; Jennie Martowska and Dino Geromini; Sophie Jakobowski (partially hidden) and Jim Janofski.

St. Peter's was a thriving parish for several decades. In the 1930s, dozens of young people attended each First Communion and Confirmation class. By 1958, however, the First Communion class had dwindled to only 13 children.

29

When the first Syrians immigrated to South Norwood, they worshiped in their homes or traveled to Boston for Sunday services. By 1918, however, the Syrian population had reached a critical mass of about 150 people, and a society was formed to raise money for a church in Norwood. Ground was broken the following year, and St. George's Syrian Orthodox Church, located on Atwood Avenue, was dedicated in 1921.

Fire destroyed the first Syrian church on Good Friday in 1933, leaving only a large wooden cross, which, according to newspaper reports, was untouched by the flames. The congregation celebrated Easter in the Balch School, and immediately set about rebuilding the church. The present church, seen above, was dedicated in 1934. Greek itinerant artist Peter Afentakis painted the murals in front of the altar.

The first Sunday school at St. George's Orthodox Church was founded in 1936 by Esther Deeb. In June 1941, six young members of the church made history as the first Syrian Orthodox Sunday school graduating class in the United States. Seen in this *c.* 1949 Sunday school photograph are, from left to right, Jackie Saloman, Donna Fanciose, Janice Howard, and Judy Campisano. Their teacher is Florence Esper.

In May 1949, the St. George's Orthodox Church Choir went on the road, singing at St. George's Church in Lawrence, a choir festival in Methuen, and on radio station WLAW. The choir was directed by Jack Bitar. Pictured here before the choir's tour are, from left to right, the following: (first row) Eleanor Tomm, Delal Assim, Joan Tomm, and Beverly Tomm; (second row) Sally Assim, Alice Esper, Esther Deeb (choir mother), Diana Bitar, and Florence Esper.

Members of St. George's Orthodox Church gather in 1962. From left to right are the following: (first row) Florence Esper, Hayes Kelley, Marshall Kelley, Rev. Nifon Abraham, Esther Deeb, Emilie Moses, Margie Thomas, George Eysie, and Sandy Thomas; (second row, beginning at top of stairs) Edward Thomas, Alice Kelley, James Bethoney, Samera Bethoney, Marty Kelley, George Thomas, Catherine Esper, Michael Mike, Samera Mike, Freda Franciosi, Dolores Elias, Beverly DiFlaminies, Julia Lewis, Charles Kelley, and Nadir Kalliel.

The Hos'n Hospital Society was founded c. 1930 and is headquartered in Pittsburgh. Even today, the society raises funds for a rural county hospital some 100 miles from Damascus, Syria. Over the years, Norwood's St. George's Orthodox Church has raised countless thousands of dollars for this worthy cause. Among the 1979 volunteers are, from left to right in the first row, Regina Boulis, Samera Mike, Mabel Bitar, Jack Bitar, Fr. Nifon Abraham, Rose Joseph, Eleanor Tomm, and Ann Thomas.

Three

HOME AND FAMILY

In 1924, a *Boston Globe* headline announced that Norwood had the highest birth rate in the state. Among the largest families were two from South Norwood: the Matsons of Cedar Street with 11 children, and the Mike family of Concord Avenue with 8 children. Many South Norwood families lived in triple-decker homes with members of their extended family, a situation that encouraged close familial ties. In this photograph, triple-decker houses line Dean Street in the 1920s.

A young Emory Richard Tomm (right) appears proud of his Norwood athletic wear in this c. 1910 photograph, as he poses with his sister Risheady Tomm (left) and their cousin John Alec Abdallah. The Tomms were the children of Syrian immigrants Habib and Damlah Tomm, who owned a handkerchief factory on Dean Street. John was the son of Nicholas and Rashede Abdallah, proprietors of South End Hardware on Washington Street.

At one time the home of George H. Morrill, owner of the Morrill Ink Works, this elaborate mansion stood on a hill overlooking Dean Street. Shortly after their arrival in Norwood, Habib and Damlah Tomm acquired the property. The family lived there for several years, and then converted the home into apartments. A grandchild of the Tomms recalls that each room in the mansion had a marble fireplace.

Amelia Lukesewicz and Louis Dauksewicz emigrated from Poland and were married in South Boston before relocating to Norwood. They are pictured here with their children, from left to right, Edward, Helen, and Vitold. Louis worked at Bird & Son, and Edward worked, for a time, at Swift's Laundry. Vitold died of heart disease at age 6. In 1941, Helen Dauksewicz married John Alec Abdallah, grandson of one of South Norwood's first Syrian immigrants.

Nick and Rose Troilo emigrated from Italy around 1915 and made their home on Talbot Avenue in South Norwood. This formal portrait was taken in a local studio c. 1919. Pictured from left to right are Violet, William, Nick, Antonio, Rose, and Jean. Antonio, a baby here, later drowned in a tragic accident at Willett Pond when he was 14.

Polish immigrants to South Norwood included Annie and Charles Bochanowicz (center), pictured here with their children, from left to right, Henry, Edwina, Alphonse, and Edmond. The Bochanowicz family lived on Tremont Street. Charles managed the Polish Cooperative Store on Washington Street and, later, worked for Bird & Son. Alphonse and Edmond died while serving in World War II. Henry and Edwina each married and raised families in South Norwood.

With parents working long hours in local factories or family businesses, children played an important role in running the household. Beverly (left) and Dolores Tomm, children of E. Richard and Sophia Tomm of Dean Street, were responsible for helping with the care of the family's animals, including these goats.

It was common practice for families in South Norwood to take in boarders to help make ends meet. Often, even those who were renters would sublet their space to a number of other boarders. Here, Stanley Matusewicz (right) of Lewis Avenue shakes hands with his second-floor tenant's boarder, who is remembered only as Mike.

Even after putting in long hours of manual labor at the factories, many South Norwood men still found themselves in need of additional income to clothe, feed, and house their families. Some supplemented their income by making home-brewed beer and moonshine, which they sold to friends and neighbors.

These neighborhood boys helped Stanley Matusewicz build a clubhouse behind his home at 16 Lewis Avenue with throw-away materials donated by Norwood Lumber and the tannery. The youngsters are pictured here, from left to right, as follows: (first row) "Porky" Ronci, Zig Martowska, Peter Stanchuk, Johnny Ronci, and Walter Martowska; (second row) Eddie Stanchuk and Tony Martowska.

A group of friends who grew up together in the Austin Street neighborhood of South Norwood celebrate on the eve of their high school graduation in 1939. From left to right are the following: (first row) Luciano Marinelli and Jimmy O'Leary; (second row) Henry Benedetti, Ann Basilici, and Fred Babel; (third row) Alphonse Bochanowicz, Julius Onichuk, and Edward Costello.

Michael and Francis Triventi, sons of Dominick and Josephine Triventi, stand outside the family home at 104 Cedar Street in 1940. The two lived on the second floor of the house with their parents, while their maternal grandmother, Filomena Tudor, resided on the first floor. For a time, the family rented third-floor rooms to boarders.

Mabel and Jack Bitar stand near their Concord Avenue home with their children, Daniel and Diana. After immigrating to the United States from Syria as a teenager, Jack was a laborer until poor health forced him to stop. Fluent in Arabic, he was a chanter at St. George's Orthodox Church for 65 years, and also helped neighbors write letters to their homeland. Jack was well known as a ticket taker at the Norwood Cinema for decades.

This aerial view shows the triple-decker flats and businesses of South Norwood in 1953. Washington Street runs horizontally through the middle of the photograph. Oolah Avenue and Cedar Street stretch between Washington Street and the railroad tracks in the background. Heaton, Sturtevant, and Dean are directly below the photographer.

Many of the first Portuguese immigrants hailed from the Arcos de Valdevez area of northern Portugal, and settled in triple-decker houses on Oolah Avenue in South Norwood. Cousins Maria (Rodrigues) DaSilva (left) and Maria DaSilva are pictured next to their Oolah Avenue home in the 1960s.

Donna Franciosi, who lived across the street from this scene, is pictured in the empty lot next to St. George's Orthodox Church, on Atwood Avenue, *c.* 1948. Houses on Austin Street are visible in the background behind her.

From left to right, George Jr. (standing), Robert, and William Cofsky (with their cousin Carol) take a break from playing to pose *c.* 1942. The boys' parents and grandfather ran a trucking company, Cofsky Express, in the 1930s and 1940s. George Jr. then operated the business as Cotter Oil Company in the 1980s. Cofsky cousins ran the American Lunch, an institution in South Norwood, for many years.

Esther (Howard) Deeb was the first child born in South Norwood of Syrian-immigrant parents. She began volunteering at St. George's Orthodox Church when she was just 16, founded the Sunday school, headed the Ladies Society, and organized the church choirs. Seen here receiving the Antonian Medal of Honor from the Orthodox Church, Deeb also taught citizenship classes, served as a Syrian-English translator, and was an unofficial advocate for newly arrived immigrants.

Born to non-English-speaking Polish immigrants, Walter J. Gotovich worked at Norwood Press, and attended law school at night. While leading a youth group, he met Anne Smolski, children's librarian at the Morrill Memorial Library and daughter of Lithuanian immigrants. In 1942, their wedding at St. George's Roman Catholic Church was one of the first Polish-Lithuanian unions in South Norwood. Walter served as town moderator and counsel from 1957 to 1972.

This row of multifamily dwellings remains in South Norwood today. Past residents remember the distinctive porches that were places for conversation, dining, and sleeping in the summer, and the well-kept yards that were often filled with vegetable gardens and fruit trees. Many people also recall how clean and carefully maintained the apartments were. Families always took a great deal of pride in their homes.

Standing under the apple tree in the backyard of 18 Folan Avenue, the home of the Gotovich family, are a group of neighborhood friends. Pictured from left to right are Perry Frangiosi, Bernadette Gotovich, Linda Stupak, Irene Gotovich, and James Gotovich. The Balch School can be seen in the background.

James and Margaret Mitchell lived in this house at the corner of Mylod and Washington Streets from 1897 to 1922. James worked as a laborer for Bird & Son in South Norwood and at the Winslow tannery, until his death in 1915. After Margaret's death, her son James Jr. and his wife, Christine, sold the house and moved to California.

South Norwood children gather in the basement of the Abdallah family home on Washington Street to celebrate spring birthdays in this 1957 photograph. Olga, Nick, and Helen Abdallah are seated at center.

Georgianna Boulis poses with flowers in her yard on Washington Street in the 1950s. In the background, across Washington Street, the homes along St. Joseph Avenue are visible. Georgianna's father, George, was a well-known barber in South Norwood. As an adult, Georgianna worked at the Norwood Town Hall for many years.

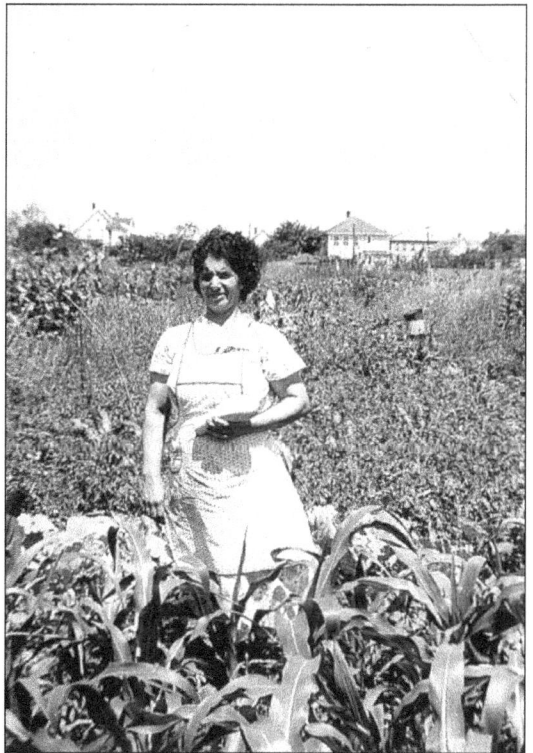

Mabel Howard Bitar stands in the community garden that was located on the site of today's Alandale Parkway. The garden became a symbol of the camaraderie that developed among residents of South Norwood, as families took advantage of the open space by planting vegetable and flower gardens. According to some, each ethnic group worked a particular portion of the land, and when the time came, all shared in the abundant harvest.

Maria and Mario Rodrigues were featured in an August 1979 *Patriot Ledger* newspaper article about their efforts to help new Portuguese immigrants acclimate to life in South Norwood. The Rodrigueses helped newcomers find housing and work, and assisted them in learning English and completing the requirements for their American citizenship. For the article, they were photographed in front of the triple-decker house they own on St. James Avenue.

Many first-generation Portuguese-Americans in South Norwood speak of the efforts their parents made to preserve their culture. For some, that meant that only Portuguese was spoken at home. For others, it meant spending summer vacations with extended relatives in Portugal. Here, neighbors Luciana Rodrigues and Bruno Liquito pose in traditional Portuguese dance clothing *c.* 1980.

Four

EARNING A
LIVING WAGE

Norwood Lumber was a successful enterprise for a number of years, with two South Norwood neighbors handling the office work. Josephine Zabrowski worked as the secretary, and Janina Pavilonis as the cashier and switchboard operator. Many South Norwood men were hired as day laborers to unload boxcars of lumber whenever a large shipment arrived by rail.

Founded by Abner Guild c. 1776, the tannery employed local residents for 175 years, making it one of the longest-running businesses in Norwood. By 1901, Winslow Brothers & Smith operated one tannery on Railroad Avenue and a second off Endicott Street. In this early photograph, laborers from the Winslow plant stand outside one of the facility's many buildings.

Both Stanley and Sophie Matusewicz were employed at the Winslow Brothers & Smith tannery off Endicott Street. The couple worked long hours in the plant, and then returned to their home where, like many of their neighbors, they cultivated a large garden.

The tanneries specialized in converting sheepskin into leather, which was then sold for the manufacture of wallets, belts, hats, gloves, and specialty products such as imitation zebra and alligator skin. Later, the Winslow plant expanded to include wool and glue departments for processing by-products of the tannery business. In 1912, Willett Pond, known locally as New Pond, was created to supply water to the tannery.

By 1935, Winslow Brothers & Smith employed 700 people in their two Norwood plants. Although the company boasted of being the first in the industry to voluntarily reduce work days to nine hours, labor disputes during the Depression brought on a series of sometimes violent strikes. A 1949 strike led to the closing of the Railroad Avenue location. The Winslow tannery on Endicott Street, seen in this aerial photograph, closed in 1952.

In 1856, Samuel Morrill moved his ink business from Andover, Massachusetts, to Norwood, setting up shop on the south end of Pleasant Street. By 1884, under the direction of son George H. Morrill, the ink works had expanded to include 14 buildings, 100 employees, and its own railroad station. The plant employed hundreds of workers from South Norwood over the years.

The George H. Morrill Company became the largest producer of printing inks in the United States by 1913. Here, in 1922, the truck signage brags of Morrill's increased production to 25 million pounds of ink per year, while still harking back to the company's modest beginnings in 1840. Morrill's merged with four other companies seven years later to create the General Printing Ink Company. Production was gradually reduced, and in 1972, the renamed Sun Chemical Corporation relocated to Mansfield.

50

Norwood Press, founded in 1894, was located on the outskirts of South Norwood. The press was actually a partnership of three independent companies: J. S. Cushing & Company, typesetting; Berwick & Smith, printing; and E. Fleming & Company, bookbinding. Neighborhood children remember receiving scrap paper from press employees. After World War I, labor disputes began to disrupt the company and eventually contributed to the closing of press operations in 1952.

Plimpton Press moved from Boston to Norwood in 1897. Noted for textbook publishing, at its peak, Plimpton's produced 50,000 volumes daily at the Lenox Street plant. During World War II, the company newsletter included many South Norwood boys on its "honor roll" of employees. Sometime after the war, Emilie Moses, a well-known South Norwood resident, became the editor of Plimpton's newsletter.

Bird & Son, one of the first paper manufacturers in New England, built a factory on the Neponset River in East Walpole in 1817. In 1904, the company opened a roofing plant on Pleasant Street in South Norwood. A floor-covering factory followed in 1911. Eventually, Bird's manufactured everything from commercial paper to flower pots. These men were among the company's early employees.

After immigrating to South Norwood, Pat Sansone encouraged Dominick Triventi, his neighbor in Italy, to come work at Bird's. Triventi did come to America and found employment in Bird's roofing plant, while Sansone worked in floor covering. Both remained at Bird's for decades. Pictured here, Josephine Tudor and Dominick Triventi (couple on left) stand up for groom Pat Sansone and bride Margaret Mitcherony (couple on right) on their wedding day. A few years later, Triventi and Tudor were also wed.

Employing more than 1,000 Norwood residents, Bird & Son claimed to be the first paper mill in Massachusetts to implement a system of three 8-hour shifts, rather than two 12-hour shifts. The plants continued to expand, and Bird's was the largest commercial taxpayer in Norwood through the 1970s. This 1929 aerial photograph shows the floor-covering plant in the foreground and the roofing plant in the background.

Apolonia Tamasunas (left) walked out of Lithuania in 1918 at the age of 18 and made her way to Norwood, where she married Peter Babel (right). Both worked at the tannery for years. Later, she worked at the Norwood Laundry, while her husband and son Fred, seen at center in his Navy uniform, found positions at Bird's. After nearly 30 years of employment, the younger Babel's pension was $5 per month.

In the early 20th century, Bird & Son bought 35 acres in Walpole and built the Bird Club House, a recreational facility for its employees. Eventually, the complex contained a billiard hall, gymnasium, ball fields, and a free-standing library building. The company sponsored a

variety of employee-run athletic associations and social activities, including ball teams and a camera club. Bird's also held annual company parties and picnics. Here, employees and their families gather on July 17, 1923, for the fifth annual company picnic.

These young men worked in the Finishing Department of the Bird & Son flooring plant in 1940. Pictured from left to right are the following: (first row) John Murphy and John Lasky; (second row) John Mitchell, Warren Smith, and John Davidonis; (third row) Frank Jankowski, Henry Houghton, John Farrell, and Howard Johnson.

Bird & Son employees participated in a golfing competition as part of a company-organized field day in July 1940. Seen here, from left to right, are the following: (first row) Velma Cobb, Muriel McDonald, Lilyan Paquette, Gladys Boulter, Julia Lewis, Martha McLauchlan, and Agnes Flood; (second row) Marion Tolman (in hat), Ann Kelliher, Margaret Delaney, and Ruth Anderson (at far right); (third row) Anne Lindsay, Catherine Delaney, Bertha Broadley, Marion Smith, Louise Geary, Mary Bannon, Hannah Flavin, and Margaret Corcoran.

Bird & Son also published an employee newsletter containing company news, reports on sports teams and clubs, and announcements of employee weddings, retirements, and vacations. In 1937, the newsletter dutifully reported that the company baseball team, pictured here, won 18, lost 13, and tied 2 games. It was, the reporter wrote, an improvement over the team's performance the previous year.

The Bird & Son softball team had a stellar season in 1940, when it took the Norwood Soft Ball League Championships by winning 22 games and losing only 2. Team members included, from left to right, the following: (first row) John Bradley, Bartley Coyne, John Heylin, Moses Bader, Coleman Coyne, and Frank Shimsky; (second row) Joseph Eppich, Leroy Walton, Thomas Miller, John Cooke, Peter Didicks, Lester Tarbell, Robert Wood, and Ernest Paciorkowski.

The Norwood Stamping Company (above), located on Lenox Street, counted many Portuguese immigrants among its 100 employees. The company manufactured paper and metal products until its closure in 2003. Lucinda DaSilva (right) worked as a machine operator at the Norwood Stamping Company for more than 20 years. She is seen here with a coworker during a lunch break on the factory floor in the 1980s.

Five

BUSINESSES
AND SERVICES

Standing at the intersection of Old Washington Street, made defunct by the railroad underpass construction in 1897, the photographer captures the center of South Norwood's business district. Seen on the right is the A&P food store and the Pickwick Ale sign that hung at Nick's (Abdallah) Package Store. On the left is the Boston Shoe Store. In the distance, smoke rises from the smokestack of Bird's central power plant.

Stretching south on Washington Street from Dean Street, this building had commercial space on the first floor and apartments on the upper levels. This image photographed for a gas company promotion shows gas stoves ready for installation. Pictured from left to right are Leo Sansone (child), Charlie Sansone (owner of the building), Bob Hathaway, Dick Champion, John Galligan, John Moloney, and Ed Roberts. Galligan, Moloney, and Roberts worked as fitters for the gas company.

These two dwellings, located on the left of Dean Street just before the railroad bridge, were utilized for commercial purposes by the Habib Tomm family beginning c. 1902. Employees traveled by trolley from Boston to work at the factory, which made handkerchiefs for railroad conductors and gloves for painters. Eventually, the Tomms closed the factory and converted the buildings into apartments.

Olga Abdallah (left) made town history in 1969 as the first woman elected to the board of selectmen. Her election was bittersweet, however, as she filled the seat vacated by the untimely death of her father, John Alec Abdallah. A fourth-generation businesswoman, Olga is pictured here in the family's South End Hardware store with customer Bertha Gregory Malpass. The store was also the site of South Norwood's first post office.

On the east side of Washington Street, Benny Koznick's Independent Furniture Company was located in the three-story brick building next to Café Venice, a neighborhood landmark. The furniture company building at one time was occupied by a spaghetti factory. South Norwood residents remember lining up to buy spaghetti by the case, which would then be divided among neighbors. This photograph was taken on the sad occasion of Nick Abdallah's funeral in 1961.

The central business district of Washington Street contained shops, businesses, and services geared toward the various ethnic groups living in the area. There were Lithuanian, Polish, Syrian, and Italian grocers, many exhibiting signs in various languages to better serve their customers. Here, two South Norwood residents share neighborhood gossip in front of Morini's Market.

Andrea DiMarzo (third from left), an Italian immigrant seen here with his wife, Josephine, and sons Alfred (far left), Charles (kneeling), and Joseph, worked as a master tailor for Hart, Schaffner, and Marx in Boston until he decided to open his own shop. He started Andy's Tailor Shop on Washington Street near Sturtevant Avenue in 1929.

Residents stand at the intersection of Oolah Avenue and Washington Street to watch a Veterans Day parade make its way through South Norwood. By the time of this mid–20th century photograph, Romano's Market had replaced Morini's on the corner.

Just across Oolah Avenue from Romano's, this Shell gas station opened for business in the mid-1900s. It was a popular gathering spot for neighborhood youths, some of whom are standing in front of the entrance. At the time, gas was priced at just under 33¢ per gallon.

These advertisements for South End Hardware and B. A. Tumavicus & Company stores were found in the 1918 Resident and Business Directory of Norwood and Walpole, Massachusetts, published by the Union Publishing Company of Boston. Both stores were mainstays of the diverse Washington Street business district.

Lithuanians, in particular, supported the grocery and provisions store of Baltramejus (B. A.) Tumavicus, located at 1147 Washington Street on the corner of Concord Avenue. Tumavicus had competition from fellow Lithuanians John Chubet and Michael Jurenas. Tumavicus also ran a coal and wood business out of this first-floor retail space.

This early–20th century photograph captures an unidentified South Norwood independent grocery store owner and his customers. Residents remember the names of several grocers and cooperative markets that sprang up in the neighborhood, including V. P. Repzis, Frank Giampietro, Elias Nassif, Joseph Howard, the South Norwood Polish Market, and the Lithuanian Cooperative Market.

South Norwood Photo Studio

Pictures Taken at Studio or at Your Home
at a Lower Price than Others.

WE DO ENLARGING and FRAMING

JOHN KLUKAS, Prop.

1 ST. JAMES AVE.,   -   -   -   -   NORWOOD

Telephone, Norwood 389-R

Many immigrants had formal portraits taken at weddings, upon the birth of a child, and even at death. These images were often the only means of sharing the happenings in their lives with members of their extended family overseas. At least two photographic studios existed in South Norwood. Alexander Lapinsky opened a studio at 1084 Washington Street, and John Klukas owned the South Norwood Photo Studio on St. James. The latter advertised in the Norwood Business Directory.

As with many family businesses in South Norwood, the trucking company Cofsky Express was a multigenerational effort. Michael Cofsky worked as a teamster for many years before opening his own company at 65 Austin Street in 1924 with his sons Frank, Simon, and George (pictured). One daughter, Anne, also worked as the company's bookkeeper. By the late 20th century, the business was operated by George's son George Jr. as the Cotter Oil Company.

DRUG **BRUZGA'S** STORE
UP-TO-DATE
WILLIAM C. BRUZGA REG. PHARM., Ph.G., Ph.C.
PRESCRIPTION SPECIALISTS

1098 WASHINGTON ST.   NORWOOD, MASS.

Saugokit savo sveikatą dabar, laike šalčių ir influenzai siaučiant. Receptus mes visuomet išpildome atydžiai ir teisingai, tad reikale ateikit pas mus, o busit patenkinti geru patarnavimu, ir teisinga kaina.

Bekernė ir sąkrova
Kepam gardžiausią lietuvišką duoną, taipgi užlaikom visokių skanumynų. Visiems patarnaujam kuogeriausia.
P. Bechunas
1226 WASHINGTON STREET
SO. NORWOOD, MASS.

P. JAKŠTYS
Savininkas.
LIETUVIŲ BARBERNĖS
Kurią visi žino už geriausį patarnavimą.
1116 WASHINGTON STREET
SO. NORWOOD, MASS.

Tarpininkas (Mediator) was a Lithuanian journal published in South Boston. The January 1929 issue was entitled "Norwoodo Numeris" (Norwood Number), a sure indication of the size and significance of the Lithuanian community in the town. Among the advertisements in the journal were these for Bruzga's Drug Store, Bechunas's Bakery, and Jakstys's Barbershop, all located on Washington Street in South Norwood.

By 1916, Sam Boulis, a Syrian immigrant, was operating a barbershop in South Norwood. His nephew George came to live with the family and, by the late 1930s, had taken over for his uncle. George Boulis is pictured here with his wife, Regina, and their daughters, from left to right, Marie, Regina, and Georgianna. The family lived above the shop at 1132 Washington Street for many years before moving to Austin Street.

Started in 1927 as part of the Woman's Club, the Norwood Women's Community Committee first opened its thrift shop on Guild Street. Over the years, the WCC has raised thousands of dollars for local relief and social service activities. In 1966, the thrift shop moved to its current South Norwood location on Washington Street, where it still thrives, operated entirely by volunteers selling donated merchandise.

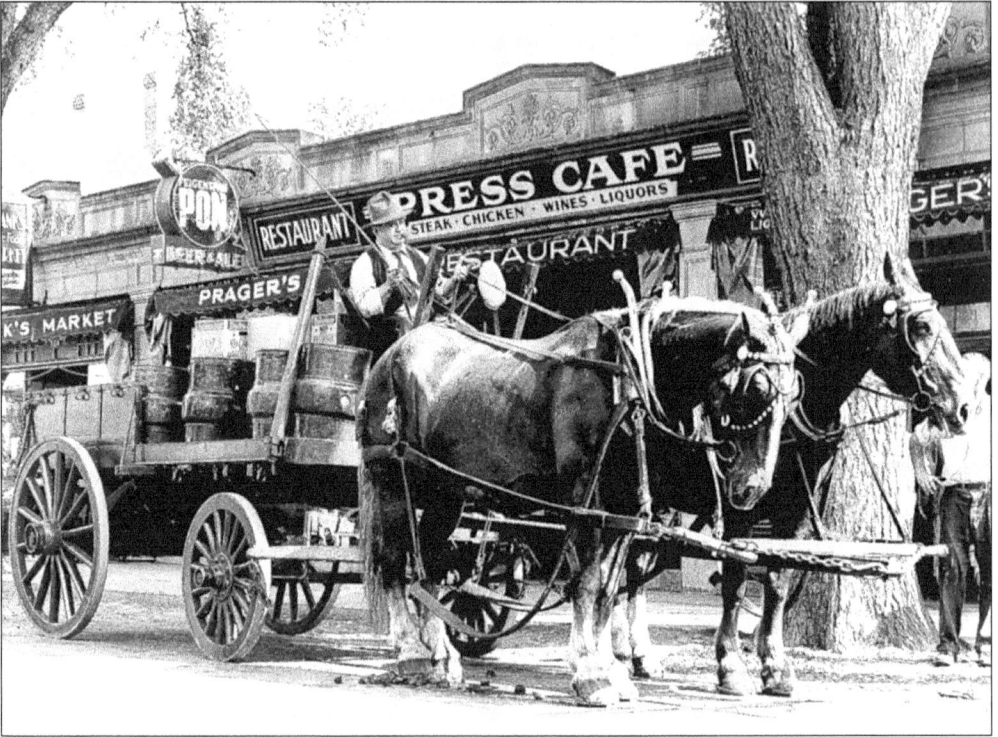

In this staged 1942 photograph, Nicholas Abdallah, proprietor of South End Hardware, moves his team and wagon along Washington Street, past his own storefront and that of the Press Café. Prager's Press Café was not simply a restaurant, but was a market as well, offering groceries, meat, and liquor. From the 1940s through the 1960s, a number of successful restaurants were located in South Norwood, including the Wingding, the Venice, and Jennie's Pizza Parlor.

Under the direction of Adam and Janina Benkavitch, Stanley's Market became one of the most popular establishments in South Norwood. Known for top-grade meats and the highest-quality fruits and vegetables, the market was also famous for its kielbasa, often called "the best in New England." Seen here in 1974, the market reflected the ethnic diversity of the neighborhood, with Italian sausages and Bacalhau being advertised.

George "Chuck" Elias was a partner in the South End Market in the 1940s, and the proprietor of Foodland beginning in 1952. In 1963, he and his wife, Dolores, opened a coffee shop and beauty salon on Washington Street at Weld Avenue. The Colonial Coffee Shoppe provided patrons with friendly service for nearly 20 years. Here, Elias stands by the counter with his wife, Dolores (far right), and daughters Dianne (second from right) and Sharon.

Born and raised in Boston, George Keegan opened the Norwood Jewelry Store in 1960. Keegan was confined to a wheelchair after contracting polio, and he learned the watch-making trade at the Massachusetts Hospital School in Canton. The little corner store at 1144 Washington Street and Keegan himself, known as "George the Jeweler," quickly became popular fixtures in the South Norwood community.

69

At the southern end of South Norwood, John and Bernard Chubet opened a grocery and variety store at the corner of Washington Street and St. Joseph's Avenue in 1924. The small storefront, seen here with the awning down, also had a soda fountain and penny-candy counter. The family operated the store until the mid-1950s, getting most summertime business from neighborhood residents on their way to Hawes Pool.

This view, looking north from Cedar Street down Washington, was photographed in 1919, when the central business district of South Norwood was coming into its own. The trolley tracks in the street and the telephone poles along Washington can be seen. The trolley tracks are now gone, but the removal of the telephone poles remains a hotly debated issue. Many South Norwood residents want the poles to be removed and replaced with buried telephone lines, as was done in "uptown" Norwood many decades before.

70

Six

ACROSS THE TRACKS TO SWEDEVILLE

Swedeville, which sprang up in the area surrounding Cedar and Chapel Streets and along Savin Avenue, was connected to South Norwood by Cedar Street. The neighborhood attracted immigrants from both Sweden and Finland beginning in the late 19th century. Encountering many of the same obstacles faced by their South Norwood neighbors, residents of Swedeville also created a close-knit, self-contained enclave.

Located at the corner of Savin and Melville Avenues, the variety store owned by Willehard Karki stood at the center of Swedeville. In this 1922 photograph, Karki stands behind his brand-new soda fountain counter. A well-known and well-liked entrepreneur, he also ran a popular poolroom at 33 Savin Avenue, across the street from the store.

This dry goods and shoe store at 39 Chapel Street was built and operated by Rev. Anders Kallgren, who also served as the minister of the Swedish Baptist Church. Anders (far left), his son Samuel, and his wife, Emma, all pictured here, lived in the apartment above the store. Later, the commercial space was rented to grocer Olavi "Whitey" Huttunen.

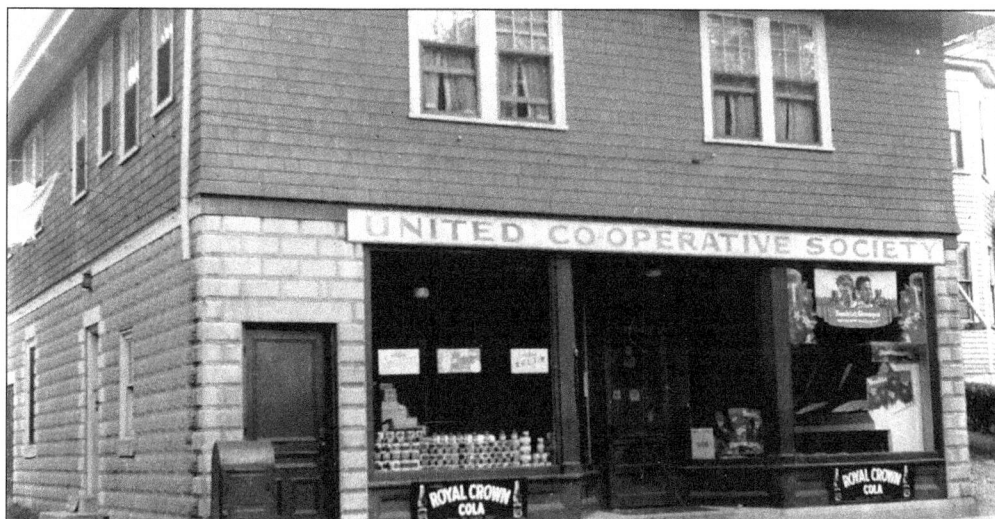

In 1909, the Finnish community of Norwood opened a cooperative store, called Turva, at the site of the first Swedish Congregational Church building on Savin Avenue. The United Cooperative Society of Norwood, as it officially became in June 1921, kept the residents well supplied. The second floor of the structure housed, at various times, a shoe store, a dry goods store, and a restaurant.

TURVA COOPERATIVE CASH GROCERY

OSCAR BAGGE, Manager

CHOICE GROCERIES

Fresh and Salt Meats and Vegetables.

47 Savin Ave., NORWOOD, MASS.

Telephone 124-M

A. KALLGREN

DRY AND FANCY GOODS   GENTLEMEN'S FURNISHINGS

Boots, Shoes and Rubbers

CONFECTIONERY, ICE CREAM, SODA

Cigars, Tobacco and Stationery.

39 Chapel St., NORWOOD, MASS.

Advertisements for the Turva Cooperative and Kallgren's store appeared in the 1918 Norwood Business Directory. The need for such neighborhood establishments declined during the 1930s and 1940s. After World War II, the Finnish society's store, the nearby milk plant, and eventually the society itself were dissolved. Kallgren's, subsequently known as Whitey's, was run as a small variety store until the early 1980s.

73

In 1903, the Finnish Workingman's Association of Norwood—called INTO—was formed, and a modest meeting hall was built off Chapel Street. A few years later, the structure was enlarged, and the organization was legally certified in part "for the purpose of promoting among the working class in Norwood a feeling of self-reliance, elevating them morally, intellectually and financially." Theater, music, and sports activities were all enthusiastically supported.

INTO's founding board of directors included, from left to right, the following: (first row) Otto Kulmala, Oscar Bagge, and Oscar Sulonen; (second row) Werner Sointu, Emil Salonen, Viktor Malmi, and Willehard Karki. As the children of these immigrants matured and were assimilated into the wider community, INTO's membership declined. In May 1959, the hall was sold to the American Legion.

Along with their three small children, Robert and Anna Lindfors arrived in the United States to stay for one year in order to care for Anna's sister Maria, who was seriously ill. Maria died within the year, but the Lindfors family made a home in Norwood and never returned to Finland.

Algot Johnson was one of many immigrants who found work in industrialized Norwood. In the early 20th century, he settled on Savin Avenue, and found employment at the Norwood Ice Company. Seen here c. 1917 with his ice wagon and horse, Johnson became "the ice man" for his Swedeville neighbors.

In 1898, the Swedish Baptists of Norwood were incorporated as part of the Swedish Baptist Church of Boston. They first held services in this small chapel on Cedar Street, just beyond the railroad tracks into South Norwood. In 1899, Anders Kallgren answered the call to serve the Norwood congregation, which then consisted of 12 people.

During the tenure of Rev. Anders Kallgren, the membership of the Swedish Baptist Church increased. Bolstered by a Sunday school, the Young People's Society, and the Missionary Circle, the congregation moved into a newly built church on Chapel Street, opposite Savin Avenue. The church remained there until the mid-20th century, when the sanctuary was moved, remodeled, and enlarged. It still stands today at the corner of Walpole and Berwick Streets.

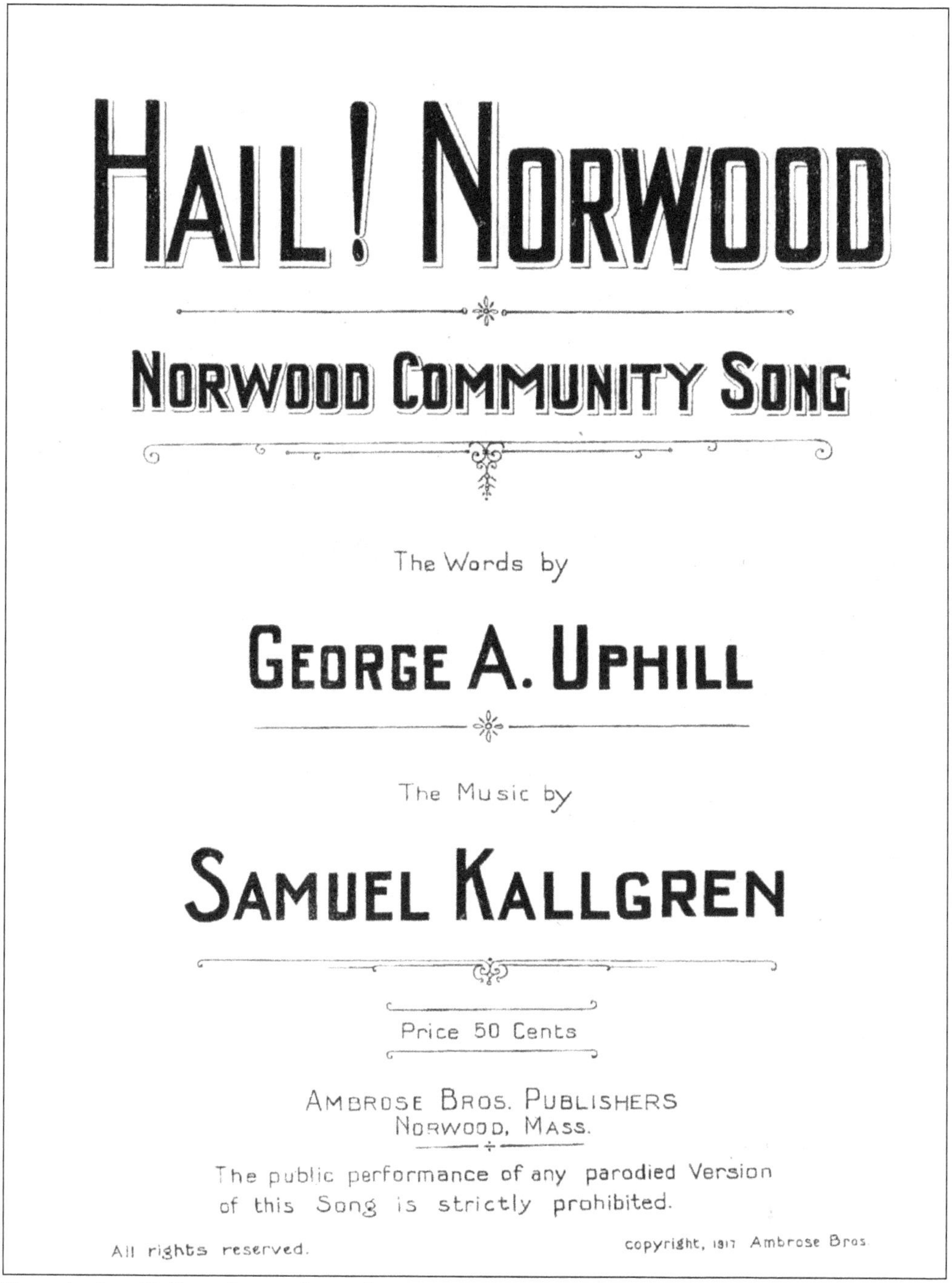

HAIL! NORWOOD
NORWOOD COMMUNITY SONG
The Words by
GEORGE A. UPHILL
The Music by
SAMUEL KALLGREN
Price 50 Cents
AMBROSE BROS. PUBLISHERS
NORWOOD, MASS.
The public performance of any parodied Version
of this Song is strictly prohibited.
All rights reserved.
copyright, 1917 Ambrose Bros.

Rev. Anders Kallgren's son Samuel grew up in Norwood, and went to work for Norwood Press. As an accomplished musician, he played violin in a quartet and became a member of the Army band during World War I. Kallgren also wrote the music for *Hail! Norwood*, a 1917 tribute to the town.

Otto Kulmala, seen in the buggy with his wife, Saima, and their three children, was one of the first board members of Finnish Hall. A staunch supporter of all hall activities, Kulmala arrived in Norwood in 1903, and worked at the Winslow Brothers tannery.

Wille Aho was a popular, well-respected young man who played a variety of roles in the neighborhood. As a businessman, he established a furniture and awning store. As a community leader, he was a tireless fund-raiser for Finnish Winter War Relief during the war years, and later became a justice of the peace, officiating at a number of Swedeville celebrations.

The Winslow Elementary School, located on Chapel Street in the Swedeville neighborhood, became a well-children's nursery during the great influenza epidemic of 1918. Here, teachers cared for the children of those who were seriously ill or had succumbed to the disease. The epidemic took a devastating toll in South Norwood and Swedeville. Perhaps ironically, the building today houses medical offices.

Proud traffic boys of the Winslow School in 1931 included several familiar Swedeville names. Ensio Hurma, Bernard Bergman, Alfons Janavich, Melville Anderson, and Howard Blasenak were all members of the group that kept the corridors of the school quiet and orderly. Several decades later, Howard's brother Walter Blasenak became Norwood's town manager.

The burning desire of young Finns to leave their homeland for the United States was often fueled by their brothers, sisters, cousins, and friends who had already made the journey. This chain migration promised the new arrivals employment opportunities and the support of pre-established social organizations. Harrskaa Joulvu and his family, seen here in a 1922 photograph, had just such a migration story.

The camaraderie of the Swedeville neighborhood was also evident in informal communal activities, called "bees." Families and friends would join together to help new arrivals build homes (house bees) and, as captured above, prepare rags for rug weaving (rag-cutting bees). While these events were a functional necessity, they were also important social gatherings, where talk of home and family prevailed.

The Swedish community in Norwood supported two additional parishes. In June 1903, the Swedish Congregational Church was founded on Savin Avenue. The group moved to a second meetinghouse on Chapel Street (right) in 1909, where it remained until the congregation disbanded c. 1939. Meanwhile, the Swedish Lutherans dedicated their first church on Cedar Street in 1899 (below). They continued to worship there for some 40 years until 1939, when a new church was erected a short distance away. Today, this Cedar Street building is the home of the Jain Center of Greater Boston.

The Siljian Lodge No. 110, Order of Vasa, was organized in 1907 as a branch of the Vasa Order of America, and it became the largest Scandinavian fraternity in Norwood. The lodge's purposes included the promotion of social and intellectual activities among its members. The children's group of the lodge had many good times, including the occasion pictured here, when the kids dressed in the costumes of various provinces of Sweden.

The Finnish band Savel, sponsored by Norwood's Finnish Hall, won several competitions and was an area favorite for many years. The band members pictured here are, from left to right, as follows (last names only): (first row) Heikkila, Maki, Wiik, director Waihela, Waihela, Ylijoki, Sointu, and Heino; (second row) Heino, Kulmala, Koski, Laakso, Kaski, and Loukko; (third row) Lindfors, Wiik, Korhonen, Sointu, and Koski; (fourth row) Matola, Koski, Rindell, Kahila, Brander, Laakso, and Sointu.

Seven

OFF TO WAR

The sons and daughters of South Norwood residents unhesitatingly signed up for military service during World War II. These six friends gathered together in South Norwood include both U.S. Army and U.S. Navy enlistees. From left to right are the following: (front) Abel Mike; (standing) Nick Grugnale, Charles Kelley, Richard Mike, George Elias, and Halem Howard. Each man also had several relatives who served in the conflict.

During World War II, Finnish Hall bustled with activity, as neighborhood women volunteered to roll bandages, knit socks and mittens, and donate hours of service for the American Red Cross. Some of the familiar Norwood faces seen here include Anna Lindfors, Anna Rindell, Anna Wuori, Liina Wiik, Ida Aho, Sylvia Niemi, and Aira Koski.

St. George's Orthodox Church also devoted time to the Red Cross, the War Bond drive, and other wartime activities. Throughout the war, the church hall was opened every Tuesday evening so that volunteers could gather and roll bandages. Here, the women commemorate their three years of making Red Cross surgical dressings. More than three dozen of the group's members donated over 100 hours to the task.

Helen Jankowski grew up on Weld Avenue in South Norwood, and was 21 years old when she enlisted in the WAVES, an acronym for Women Accepted for Volunteer Emergency Service, a U.S. Navy program instituted in 1942. She served three years, stationed in Oklahoma and the Great Lakes area. In the service, Helen met her husband, Joe Balen, and they returned to South Norwood to marry at St. Peter's Church in 1947.

Zigmund Martowska of Lewis Avenue joined the army during the war. As part of the Troop E 22nd Constabulary Squadron, he was responsible for supervising border patrols, roadblocks, and checkpoints. He was also part of the constabulary squadron during the Nuremburg Trials and was issued a World War II Victory Medal and an Army of Occupation Medal.

The gravestone of Cpl. Frederick P. Deeb, the son of Esther J. Deeb of Cedar Street, stands in Highland Cemetery. Corporal Deeb was killed while serving with the Marine Corps in the Pacific theater, and his body was among the first contingent of war dead to be returned from overseas. Corporal Deeb's body lay in state in the municipal building's Memorial Hall as a symbolic gesture to commemorate all fallen heroes.

William P. Kazulis, an 18-year-old naval aviation radioman, third class, was mortally wounded during a "glide" bombing strike on Japanese-held Wake Island. Still, he manned and fired the tunnel gun until clear of the target before succumbing to his wounds. He was buried at sea from the stern of the *Essex* on October 6, 1943.

Sgt. Edmond Bochanowicz, a U.S. Army Air Corps mechanic and the son of Mr. and Mrs. Charles Bochanowicz of Hartford Avenue, was killed in a bomber crash at Camp Gowen, Idaho, on his mother's birthday in 1942. Annie Bochanowicz received word of her son's death on the same day that his birthday present and congratulatory letter to her arrived.

The son of Rose Bader of Sturtevant Avenue, Sgt. Naimi Bader was one of four brothers to serve during the war. A gunner in the U.S. Air Force, Naimi was reported killed in May 1943, when his plane was shot down over Germany. He had taken part in numerous successful raids over Axis Europe prior to his death. Brothers Moses, Nicholas, and William returned home safely.

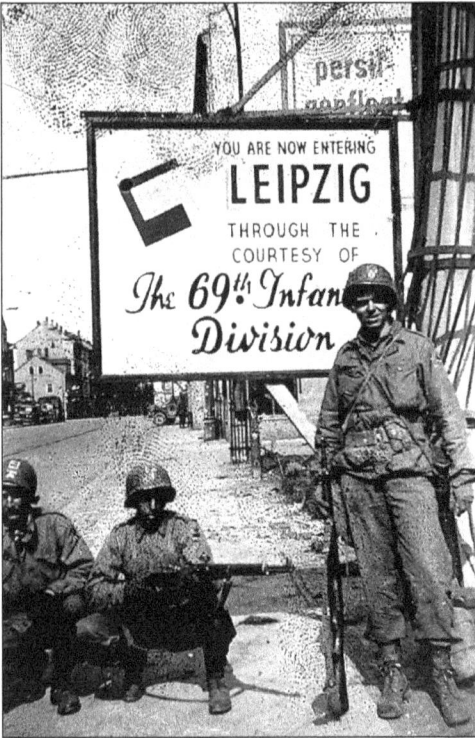

Five Elias brothers—George, Lutvie, Louis, Charles, and Michael—all members of St. George's Orthodox congregation, served in World War II. Lutvie Elias, shown here outside Leipzig in front of a banner celebrating the city's liberation, was in an anti-tank company in the 271st Infantry. He saw action throughout Europe, received a Good Conduct Medal, and was issued a Combat Infantrymen's Badge.

Adam P. Smolski, the son of Frances and Michael Smolski, Lithuanian immigrants, joined the army right out of high school at the age of 18. He saw considerable action in the European theater while serving in Company L, 328th Infantry Regiment, 26th Infantry Division, in Patton's Third Army, and was awarded a Bronze Star.

Alphonse Babel served as an infantryman with Company C of the 36th Infantry Division. Babel saw action at Normandy and throughout the European theater, earning a Purple Heart with two oak-leaf clusters, a Good Conduct Medal, and a Distinguished Unit Badge.

Sgt. Michael Triventi (right), the son of Dominick and Josephine Triventi of Cedar Street, was crew chief with the air force's 354th Pioneer Mustang Fighter Group. He was responsible for the maintenance of planes that included the *Skibbereen* piloted by Jim Keane (left). Sergeant Triventi was awarded the Bronze Star for maintaining aircraft that flew 100 missions or more without a mechanical abort, a goal he achieved during the Normandy invasion.

Memorial corners, individual plaques in honor of those who lost their lives in times of war, are erected near a serviceman's Norwood residence at the request of family members. At the corner of St. James Avenue and Washington Street is the plaque honoring Midshipman Peter J. Smith, who was lost when his ship was hit and sunk by an enemy submarine. Smith was 22 years of age.

Sgt. Ahti Wuori, an aerial gunner on a B-24 Liberator aircraft, was lost while on a combat strike against a Japanese fleet in Brunei Bay, northwest Borneo. After his plane suffered severe damage from anti-aircraft fire, a radio message indicated the crew was bailing out. Searches turned up no survivors. Sergeant Wuori is believed to be the last Norwood man to have died during World War II.

90

An oft-overlooked memorial to World War II veterans stands next to St. George's Roman Catholic Church on St. James Avenue. The dedication ceremony took place on August 15, 1949, the holy day of the Blessed Virgin Mary. A large number of people paid tribute to the 152 parishioners who had served in the war and the 7 who had given their lives.

One of the veterans whose name is engraved on the monument pictured above is Ens. John W. Minkevitch of Folan Avenue. After earning his "wings of gold" at the Pensacola, Florida, Naval Air Training Center, he served on the USS *Lexington* in the Pacific. Ensign Minkevitch survived the war but was killed in an automobile accident near his base in Corpus Christi, Texas.

While stationed in Hawaii during World War II, Sgt. Charlie Santoro placed this notice in the "Miss Fix-it's" column of the *Honolulu Advertiser*: "I know there are about a dozen or so people from Norwood, Massachusetts, on this rock. I wish you could call them together on Christmas Day between 1100 and 1200 at the Victory USA. I'll buy their dinner." Fourteen men, many from Santoro's own South Norwood neighborhood, accepted the invitation. The group included, from left to right, the following: (kneeling) Bill Stanewick, Michael Folan, George Tomm, A. Gugliotta, Sergeant Santoro, Clifford Waite, Walter Sword, and Wesley McManus; (standing) Michael Elias, Pat Walsh, A. Bolway, E. B. Armour, J. Colantonio, J. F. Fitzgerald, and R. Eklund. The men enjoyed a gala reunion and swapped stories of home.

Eight

CITIZENS AND STUDENTS

Identified as one of the oldest schoolhouses in Norwood, the "Old Brick School," as it came to be known, was built c. 1800. The mansard roof was a later addition. Children of the earliest South Norwood residents would have attended class in this building. Now dwarfed by neighboring commercial buildings, the schoolhouse still stands on the corner of Pleasant and Sumner Streets.

Lithuanian immigrant Vincas Kudirka recalls that when he arrived in South Norwood the area consisted of about 14 houses, farmland, and a small schoolhouse called the Balch School. Named for Rev. Thomas Balch, the first pastor of the Congregational church in South Dedham, this clapboard building served the southern precinct's children from 1867 until it was razed in 1913.

An elderly veteran stands outside the Balch School 40 years after the end of the Civil War, along with Agnes Curtin and her pupils. Miss Curtin was herself the eldest child of Irish immigrants and the first in her family to go on to higher education. In addition to teaching first grade for many years, she was also the Americanization teacher for the parents of many of her students.

94

In this 1909 photograph of Agnes Curtin and her Balch School pupils, each child is identified by name and ethnicity. Class members are, from left to right, as follows: (first row) Walter Virginski, Polish; Samuel Howard, Syrian; Frank Vietze, German; Julia Clem, Lithuanian; Ingeborg Anderson, Norwegian; and Emma Pennington, English; (second row) Thomas Connolly, Irish; Elvin Young, American; Alvah Svenson, Swedish; Arthur Michetti, Italian; Edward Pinkul, Lithuanian; Mabel Murison, Scottish; and Samuel Goldberg, Hebrew.

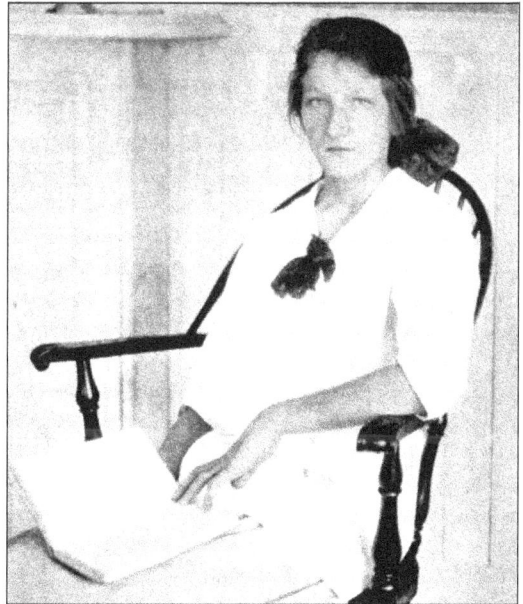

In 1918, Julia Clem, one of the girls in the previous photograph, was a high school freshman. She was also a member of the Girls' Canning Club, which was connected with the junior extension service of the Amherst Agricultural College. Some 74 girls, ages 10 to 18, joined the wartime effort to conserve food products. Clem canned 200 quarts of fruits and vegetables, including 35 quarts of blueberries she had picked herself.

From its founding, the Balch School enrolled pupils of various nationalities. Conscious of this diversity, school administrators encouraged students to embrace their ethnicity. Here, at a 1909 school fair, children and their families dress in the costumes of their native lands, and proudly hold the flags of their countries of origin, which included Italy, Lithuania,

Russia, and Finland. As the 20th century progressed, the small wooden schoolhouse could not meet the needs of the growing population of South Norwood, and plans were made to build a more substantial, modern school on the same site.

The "New" Balch School, an impressive brick edifice with striking triangular gables on its two wings, was formally accepted by the town in November 1913. It was erected well back from the street, behind the former schoolhouse, which was then razed, leaving a substantial expanse of lawn and gardens. Since then, the school has had several additions, and it remains a focal point of the South Norwood neighborhood.

One of the first classes to enter the "New" Balch School poses for a photograph at the side entrance to the building. Many of these young scholars would become members of Norwood High School's Class of 1927, while others would leave school to join the workforce.

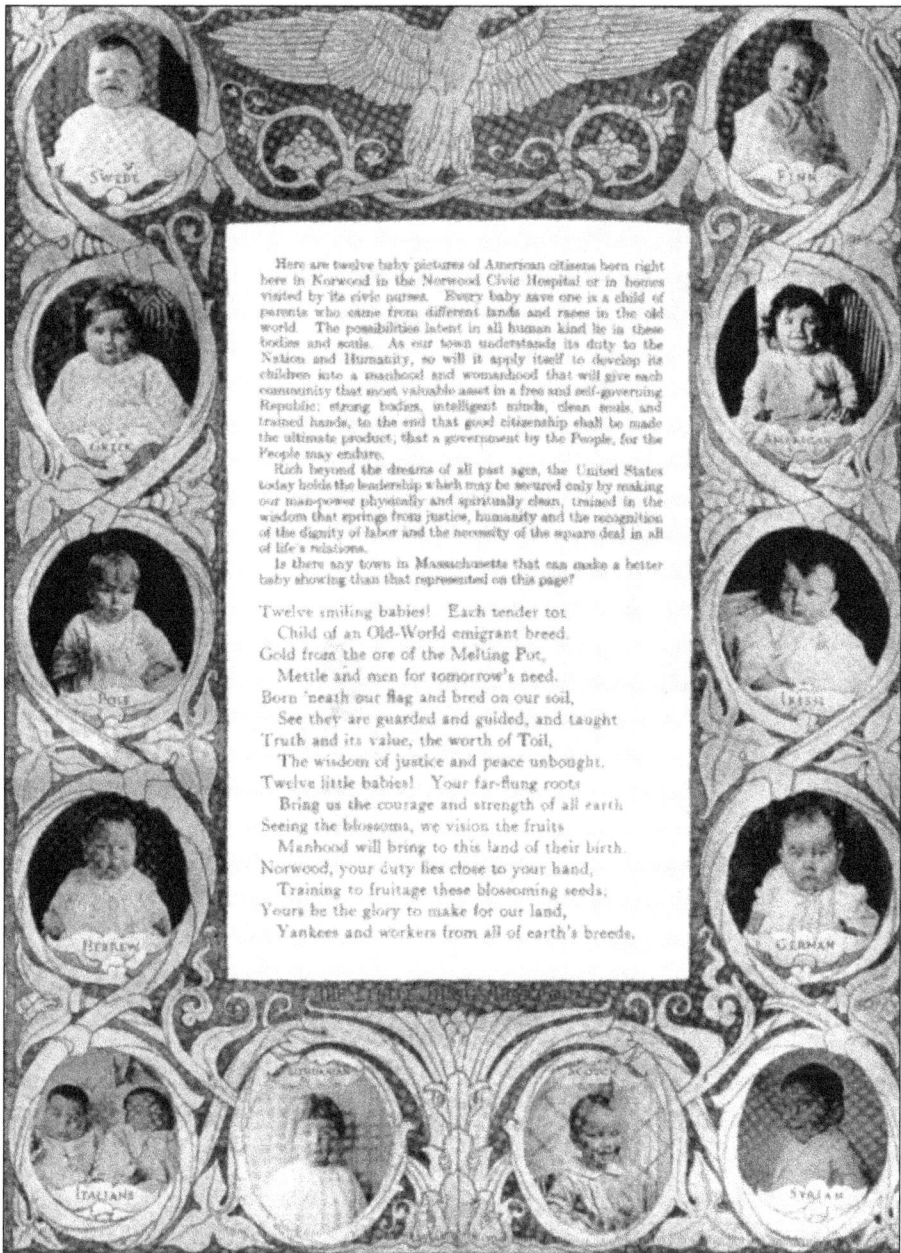

Within the illustration:

Here are twelve baby pictures of American citizens born right here in Norwood in the Norwood Civic Hospital or in homes visited by its civic nurses. Every baby save one is a child of parents who came from different lands and races in the old world. The possibilities latent in all human kind lie in these bodies and souls. As our town understands its duty to the Nation and Humanity, so will it apply itself to develop its children into a manhood and womanhood that will give each community that most valuable asset in a free and self-governing Republic; strong bodies, intelligent minds, clean souls, and trained hands, to the end that good citizenship shall be made the ultimate product, that a government by the People, for the People may endure.

Rich beyond the dreams of all past ages, the United States today holds the leadership which may be secured only by making our man-power physically and spiritually clean, trained in the wisdom that springs from justice, humanity and the recognition of the dignity of labor and the necessity of the square deal in all of life's relations.

Is there any town in Massachusetts that can make a better baby showing than that represented on this page?

Twelve smiling babies! Each tender tot
    Child of an Old-World emigrant breed.
Gold from the ore of the Melting Pot,
    Mettle and men for tomorrow's need.
Born 'neath our flag and bred on our soil,
    See they are guarded and guided, and taught
Truth and its value, the worth of Toil,
    The wisdom of justice and peace unbought.
Twelve little babies! Your far-flung roots
    Bring us the courage and strength of all earth
Seeing the blossoms, we vision the fruits
    Manhood will bring to this land of their birth.
Norwood, your duty lies close to your hand,
    Training to fruitage these blossoming seeds;
Yours be the glory to make for our land,
    Yankees and workers from all of earth's breeds.

Founded in 1912 by Norwood's greatest benefactor, George Willett, the Norwood Civic Association offered athletic programs, health services, vocational training, and entertainment to all Norwood residents. One of the organization's stated aims was to "Americanize" the immigrants in South Norwood. To that end, a 1918 issue of the *Civic Herald* contained this remarkable illustration, "The Little Things That Count." The image identifies the nationality of each of the 12 newborns, clockwise from the upper right: "Finn, American, Irish, German, Syrian, Scotch, Lithuanian, Italians, Hebrew, Pole, Greek, and Swede." The editors have also included a few inspirational paragraphs and a patriotic poem that closes with the lines, "Norwood, your duty lies close to your hand, Training to fruitage these blossoming seeds; Yours be the glory to make for our land, Yankees and workers from all of earth's breeds."

Flora Wade took her sixth-grade Balch School class on a field trip to see Boston's historic landmarks in 1928. Here, the students, along with Miss Wade (center front), enjoy a ride on the swan boats in the Boston Public Garden.

These Balch School first-graders proudly show off hats and sashes they created in art class. Although not all of these students are identified, the group includes Michael Triventi, Bertha Kaleil, Tony Calderone, George Elias, Rocco Molinari, and Michael Mike.

In 1931, fifth-graders at the Balch School were divided into teams in a dental-care competition. Those to be congratulated for having "perfect teeth" included, from left to right, Michael Triventi, Robert Gordon, Emma Giandominico, an unidentified boy, and Regina Osepovitch. Norwood children could visit the school dentist, Dr. Timothy Curtin, for 50¢. Dr. Curtin was the younger brother of teacher Agnes Curtin.

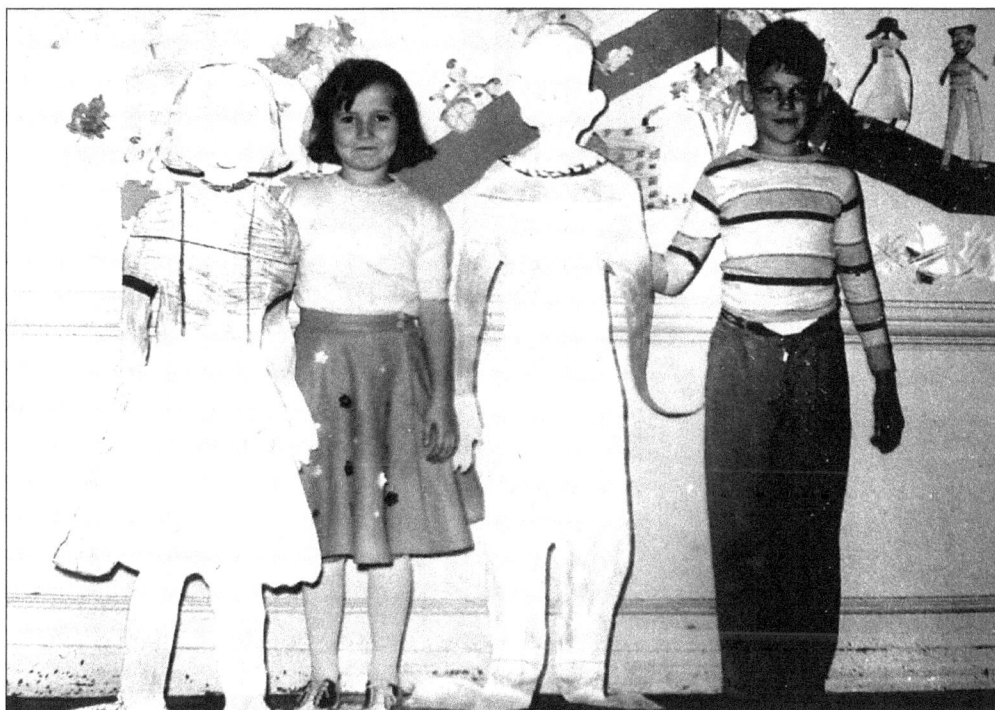

Always an innovator, the Balch School's Miss Mary Ellen O'Grady introduced her second-grade class to the fine art of making life-sized cutouts of themselves in 1955. Here, Irene Gotovich and James Balutis proudly stand beside their finished projects.

Wally Martowska and his sister Agnes (and their father in the background) stand in the backyard garden of their Lewis Avenue home in 1940. Wally wears his Balch School patrol boy sash. Patrol boys escorted the younger children from the school to their homes, ensuring their safety in crossing the streets of South Norwood.

Following the request of neighborhood residents and the South Norwood Merchants Association, the South Norwood branch of the Morrill Memorial Library was opened in a storefront at 1163 Washington Street in 1941. More than 100 people attended the Open House Day. In 1945, the branch was moved to larger quarters in the Howard Building (seen here) on Washington Street, where it remained until the early 1970s.

Inside the South Norwood branch library, Edna Phillips, Morrill Memorial Library director (standing left), and Mary Knowles, South Norwood branch librarian (standing right), assist patrons. In 1953, Knowles was subpoenaed by the Senate Internal Security Subcommittee in Washington, D.C. Knowles was fired from her job after she was accused of being a communist by FBI informant and counterspy Herbert Philbrick. In June 1960, the Court of Appeals for the District of Columbia dismissed the indictment.

This Balch School class, visiting the branch library, eventually became part of the Norwood High School Class of 1971. Class members included Paul Peswick, Robert Ciaccio, Richard Erdman, Judith Adair, Donna Rempelakis, Rayme Eysie, Ronald Mike, Mary Rizzo, and Dennis Cashman. Overseeing story time is Mrs. Doris Allen, South Norwood branch librarian.

In April 1987, Girl Scouts from the Balch School and their chaperones took a week-long trip to Washington, D.C. Helen Abdallah Donohue, one of the chaperones, remembers that the entire trip, including luxury motor coach, hotels, and tours, only cost each participant $125. The entire group was photographed on the steps of the Capitol.

The Balch School's now-annual Space Day began in 2001 with NASA's Signatures in Space project, in which photographic negatives of student-signed posters were sent on a shuttle mission. The original poster, with a certificate of authenticity, was returned to the school. Space Day also included tours of state police and local television station helicopters, and other activities on the school's playing fields.

Nine

COMPETITION AND
CAMARADERIE

The Southern Theatre, located on Washington Street, was a popular gathering spot for South Norwood residents, as well as an employer for generations of teenagers. The theater was owned by the Hayes family, who also allowed community groups to meet there. Many people fondly recall "dish nights" at the Southern, evenings when those in attendance received plates, cups, and saucers to add to a set.

Helen Wraga (left) and Vera Zabrowski are seated on the wall surrounding the Fish Pond in 1941. Located behind today's Hawes Pool, the pond area also had a bathhouse and plenty of room for picnics. Residents of South Norwood enjoyed many summer days and evenings there.

Finnish Hall's team won the title of New England Calisthenics Champions for 1930–1931. Although not all of the girls in this photograph are identified, team members include the following: (first row) Aira Koski, Irene Palonen, Lily Karki, Dorothy Heikkila, Vellamo Harju, and Salme Kuusela; (second row) Anya Salmi, Anna Lindfors, Eleanora Kkuusela, Sylvia Niemi, and Esther Kaski; (third row) Lily Kivela, Grace Anderson, Marie Koivu, Elin Aarnio, Aili Sulonen, Aino Heikkila, Aino Sulonen, and Aili Kulmala.

Live theater was a popular entertainment in Swedeville, since many immigrants had received dramatic training in their homeland. When the INTO Finnish Hall started an actors' club, it quickly attracted members who participated as actors, writers, directors, and stage builders in very professional productions. The INTO's 1925 Drama Club included director Kuuno Sevander (seated center).

Viktor Tobias Kuusela lived on Savin Avenue. Between 1920 and 1923, he won one gold medal and two silver medals in Greco-Roman wrestling for his Finnish Hall team in regional competitions. The hall sponsored many such contests at home and at clubs throughout New England. Matches could take hours to complete.

Lithuanian Hall was dedicated on St. George Avenue in 1914. Built by Lithuanian freethinkers, it was the site of socialist, communist, and radical rallies. The building also served as a makeshift morgue during the influenza epidemic of 1918, and was raided during the anticommunist Palmer Raids of 1920. Later, it was a popular location for wrestling matches and, eventually, wedding receptions. For a time, the second floor housed the popular Butterfly Ballroom.

LIETUVOS IR VILNIAUS
GARSINIAI
Krutamieji Paveikslai

Rengia SLA. 131 Kuopa

KETVERGE

Vasario-February 16, 1933

Lietuvių Svetainēje

St. George Ave.   Norwood, Mass.

Pradžia 7:30 val. vakare.

Pirmu kartu pamatysite iš Lietuvos ir Vilniaus garsinius krutamus paveikslus. Matysite SAMANOTĄ BAKUŽIĄ, kurioj jaunystēs dienas praleidom, žalią girialią ir girdēsite joje skambančias dainas. Matysite rugiapiutę ir šienapiutę. Taipgi gražiausius vaizdus, bažnyčias, karo muzējaus vēliavos nuleidimo ceremonijas, Nemuną, miestus, šventes, laidotuves, prezidentą, kariuomenę ir jos gyveniną ir taip toliaus.

Pamatysite musų SOSTINĘ VILNIŲ, kaip ji atrodo po lenkais. Vilniaus kalnelius, lietuvių įstaigas pilių gruvēsius ir kitus įdomius dalykus.

Vietos ir apielinkes lietuviai pamatykite šiuos paveikslus, visi busite patenkinti. Paveikslus fotografavo ir rodys

J. Januškevičius, Jr.   Kviečia Rengējai.

Įžanga 35c. Vaikams 15c.

The promoters of a film to be shown at Lithuanian Hall in 1933 promised that, for many, it would be "the first time they shall see moving pictures with sound." Viewers could look forward to scenes of the rye harvest and hay mowing, the beautiful scenery of their homeland, churches, cities, castle ruins, the hills of Vilnius, and Lithuanian institutions. In addition "resounding folksongs" would be heard.

Anton Koivisto Birch, a Swedeville resident, is seen here in 1916 after he won the gold medal of the New England Amateur Athletic Union in Greco-Roman wrestling. Another Finnish immigrant, John Maki, who was an auxiliary police officer and a blacksmith for the Norwood Public Works Department, traveled to Nebraska and won the world lightweight championship in Greco-Roman wrestling in 1914.

One of Norwood's finest athletes was the highly versatile John Dixon. The son of Lithuanian parents, Dixon excelled in basketball, baseball, and football and went on to play two sports at Boston College. He also tried his hand at semi-professional baseball and even heavyweight boxing in the 1930s. Dixon is seen here, seated fourth from the left, with his Norwood basketball teammates and coach H. Bennett Murray.

The Young Men's Syrian Association of St. George's Orthodox Church sponsored an adult baseball team that played against groups from the Knights of Lithuania, the Tammany Club, Bird & Son, and squads from Boston, Lawrence, and beyond during the 1930s and 1940s. Team members included, from left to right, the following: (first row) Ralph Abbott, Jimmy Kelley, and George Abbott; (second row) Ernie Deeb, John Howard, Jimmy Elias, George Bader, Bunny Thomas, and Sam "Tiger" Thomas; (third row) Tommy Elias, Eddie Thomas, Fred Selwyn, and Howard Elias. Both John Howard and George Bader were versatile athletes who had been all-scholastic football players at Norwood High in 1933.

John Howard was an outstanding athlete at Norwood High School during the 1930s, starring in football, baseball, basketball, and track. He was named all-scholastic by several area newspapers. During World War II, Howard served in the U.S. Air Force and, upon his return, rose to the rank of deputy fire chief for the town of Norwood. In 1991, he was inducted into the Norwood Boosters Club Hall of Fame.

Peter Santoro trained at Harco Murphy's Gym in South Norwood and won the New England Amateur Heavyweight Boxing Championship in 1938. Here, Santoro (far right) is pictured with two fellow marines as they take a break from boxing at their Marine Corps camp. During World War II, Santoro served in the Pacific and was awarded three Purple Hearts, including two for service on Iwo Jima. In later years, he started Roll-Land roller skating rink in Norwood with his brothers Charlie and John.

The Italian American Lodge No. 1235, affiliated with the Sons of Italy Grand Lodge, was founded in 1923 to unite in a social and civic way all people of Italian descent. Always active in cultural and charitable causes, the group also sponsored a junior lodge for boys and girls. Here, the 1932 Sons of Italy Junior Lodge girls drill team poses in front of the Balch School.

Lending their assistance during the Morrill Memorial Library's relocation from one storefront to another in 1945 are, from left to right, Boy Scouts Joseph Peatie, Richard Lee, Julian Borowko, and Edward Maini. Among the subjects most in demand at the branch library were materials on parental interests, trades, personal development, easy English for adults, and books in Russian, Lithuanian, and Polish.

Constructed at the direction of George Willett to provide water for the Winslow Brothers & Smith tannery in 1912, Willett Pond, known locally as New Pond, was a family gathering spot until the area was sold to the Archdiocese of Boston in 1963. In this photograph, members of the Howard and Boulis families cool off on a hot summer day. The bathhouse and concession stand are visible in the background.

The Hawes Brook Swimming Pool opened in June 1949. Built at a cost of $20,000 and holding 200,000 gallons of water, the pool originally had no modern filtering system, so it had to be closed, drained, cleaned, and refilled weekly. The pool became so popular that when a drought hit in August, it was deemed exempt from a townwide water ban. By the 1970s, more than 500 Norwood children were taking swimming lessons each summer at the pool.

In October 1956, St. George's Orthodox Church hall was opened for what had become an annual event, a Halloween party for the youngsters in the congregation. As in previous years, more than 100 costumed children attended. After admiring one another's costumes and playing a number of lively games, the young people enjoyed refreshments.

On February 23, 1972, Norwood celebrated its first 100 years with a centennial banquet at Roll-Land. Celebrating this gala occasion were, from left to right, the following: (seated) George Elias, Dolores Elias, Helen Abdallah, Beverly DeFlaminis, Samuel DeFlaminis, and Helen Abdallah Donohue; (standing) Olga Abdallah, Alan Danovitch, Paul Donohue, Samera Mike, and Michael Mike.

The 1973 Mardi Gras show produced by the Norwood Italian Ladies Lodge No. 1690 was a real crowd-pleaser. Members of the men's lodge joined in presenting the novelty show, which included musical and comedy acts. Lena Triventi (left, with microphone) was mistress of ceremonies and director of the show. Founded in 1933, the Eleonora Duse Lodge, named after the famous Italian actress, held meetings at Lithuanian Hall in the early 1970s.

The Ladies Society at St. George's Orthodox Church helped support the church and community by organizing social events and fund-raisers. Pictured here are members who were involved in organizing the group's Harvest Moon Dance in 1976. From left to right are the following: (first row) Alice Kelley, Helen Campisano, Ollie Abdallah, Dolores Elias, and Lovee Thomas; (second row) Helen Donohue, Beverly DiFlaminies, Nancy Deeb, Linda Thomas, Eleanor Tomm, Phyliss Solomon, Genevieve Ayoub, Emiline Eakle, and Sharon Elias.

The Rancho Folclorico do Alto Minho (Alto Minho Portuguese Folk Dance Group) was founded in 1985 by Portuguese immigrants who wanted to teach traditional music and dance to their children and grandchildren. Named after the Minho region in the north of Portugal, from whence many of the South Norwood Portuguese emigrated, the group includes more than 50 musicians, singers, and dancers who rehearse weekly at the South Norwood Portuguese Club.

Before the Portuguese community in South Norwood had established its own folk dance group, several local residents belonged to a dance group from Cambridge. Alberto DaSilva (center, with sideburns and hat) performed with the Cambridge group in a Fourth of July parade through South Norwood in 1976.

Ten

A Proud Heritage,
a Bright Future

In 2003, Balch Elementary School third-graders and teacher Michelle Wood took a walking tour of some of the town's historic sites and municipal offices. Here, class members gather at the Norwood Town Hall.

The South Norwood Improvement Association, founded in June 1938 for the purposes of enhancing the area and improving the quality of life in the neighborhood, was reactivated in 1980 as the South Norwood Committee. The group's accomplishments include reviving a neighborhood crime-watch program, organizing an annual fishing derby at Hawes Brook, and donating to worthy local causes. Here, the committee presents a donation to the Norwood Food Pantry.

South Norwood is still a neighborhood of small businesses and multifamily homes. Many of today's triple-deckers have been family owned for generations and are still maintained with a great deal of pride. In an age when many people no longer know their neighbors, South Norwood retains the sense of a village where family and friends watch out for one another.

The Howard Building on Washington Street was built by Abdallah Joseph Howard in 1918. At various times, the building housed a pool hall, a store, and the South Norwood branch of the Morrill Memorial Library. In 1938, Abdallah's son Frederick started the Howard Insurance Company. Since the 1970s, Frederick's son Andrew has been running the insurance company; his brother Philip joined the business in 1990.

South Norwood natives Martin "Minty" Kuporatz (center) and Pete Wall (right) were honored in May 2004 when two playing fields at the Balch School were named after them. Wall coached baseball at Norwood High School for 35 years, and Kuporatz worked for the Norwood Recreation Department and coached Little League and Pop Warner baseball. Here, former town selectman Joe Curran congratulates the two during the dedication ceremony.

The South Norwood Committee organized a neighborhood crime watch in 1998. Committee members pictured with Selectman Gary Lee in front of the Hawes Pool Park are, from left to right, Eleanor Brylinski, Dolores Elias, Olga Abdallah, Samera Mike, and Frances Costello. Brylinski, a dedicated volunteer for many years, had a nearby park named in her honor.

Beginning in the 1980s, the children and grandchildren of South Norwood's Portuguese immigrants attended a Portuguese after-school program that met twice per week at the Balch School. Instructors taught children Portuguese language, music, theater, and dance, and performed in traditional dress. This photograph of members of the Portuguese School and the Portuguese Folk Dance Group was taken in Walpole's Bird Park c. 1990.

120

Principals George Usevich (left) and Michael Czyryca declare their pride in their South Norwood roots. Each has a history in the neighborhood. Czyryca attended the Balch School, and Usevich's grandparents ran a market on Washington Street. Usevich and Czyryca have risen through the ranks of the Norwood public schools, and they currently lead Norwood High School and Cleveland Elementary School, respectively.

A longtime South Norwood business is the Norwood Trading Post, located next to the Balch School. John Correia and his wife started the antiques and used-furniture store in 1946 after the landmark Wingding closed its doors. For a time, the couple lived in the apartment above the store. Correia ran the same advertisement for his store in a local newspaper for more than 50 years until the ad's weekly price, which had started at $2, reached $50.

The Amazing Vase Flower Shop stands in the storefront once occupied by the American Lunch. Founded by Frank and Barbara Cofsky in the 1930s, the American Lunch, a neighborhood restaurant and bar, was a popular spot for workers from nearby facilities. As recently as the 1990s, a patron could get a corned beef and cabbage dinner there for $4.50. Amazing Vase, owned by Frani Sarantos, seen here, opened its doors in July 2003.

Boston Beef, a meat and fish market, shares the 1216 Washington Street building with Amazing Vase. Previously the site of a succession of small businesses, this location has been home to Boston Beef since 1966 and has been owned by Michael and Lisa Quinn since 1989.

Some of the newest residents in South Norwood are served by the bilingual staff at the Neighborhood Market & Deli at 1101 Washington Street. Proprietor Frank DeCosta, himself of Portuguese and Brazilian descent, says many of his customers are Brazilian immigrants who come for the imported food and specialty products he carries.

The Kraw-Kornack Funeral Home is one of the South Norwood businesses that is still family owned and operated. The business was started around 1947 by Paul H. Kraw who, as legend has it, used to sit on a hammock in front of the funeral home and chat with neighbors and passers-by. George Kornack joined the business in 1969, and now runs the funeral home in South Norwood with his son.

In 1960, George Keegan opened for business in a small corner storefront on Washington Street, and became known as "George the Jeweler." Now, 44 years later, the Norwood Jewelry Store has moved across the street to 1152 Washington, but the business remains in the family. George's son Sean (left) owns and operates the store today.

St. George's Roman Catholic Church responded to the changing demographics in South Norwood by embracing the growing number of Portuguese immigrants. These children were photographed during a festival celebrating Our Lady of Fatima at St. George's in May 2004. The day began with a parade through town, then Mass, and a celebration in the church hall. During the festival, the Portuguese Folk Dance Group performed in traditional costumes.

In spring 2004, Rev. William L. Wolkovich (pictured here) and parishioners of St. George's Roman Catholic Church received notice from the Archdiocese of Boston that the church was among 65 in the Greater Boston area that were scheduled to close. Father Bill, as he is affectionately known by young and old alike, is a modern renaissance man. A fine violinist who often utilized music in his church services, Wolkovich earned a master's degree in American studies from Boston College. In addition to his heavy workload as pastor, he devoted nearly all his free time to religious and ethnic historical research and writing. His publications include countless articles, book reviews, encyclopedic entries, and nine books, including the magisterial, three-volume *Lithuanian Religious Life in America*. In 2004, Wolkovich was awarded an honorary doctorate from Vytautas Magnus University in Kauas, Lithuania. Well loved by his parishioners and the townspeople, Father Bill retired in June 2004 after 21 years of service to South Norwood. More than 400 people attended his farewell Mass and reception.

St. Peter's Roman Catholic Church on St. Joseph Avenue was closed in 1997 as part of the Archdiocese of Boston's consolidation plans. A few years later, local son Joseph Eysie purchased the building. At the time this book went to press, Eysie was developing plans to convert the former church into condominiums. Above is an artist's sketch of the planned condos.

With the 1997 closure of St. Peter's and the 2004 shutdown of St. George's Roman Catholic Church, St. George's Orthodox Church has become the only functioning church in South Norwood. The congregation of 250 is guided by Rev. Joseph Kimmett (left), pictured here with Rev. Nifon Abraham, pastor emeritus, at a recent Easter service. The church choir, Sunday school, and Ladies Group are still active parts of the church community.

In 2001, a group of Norwood citizens successfully petitioned the town to preserve the George H. Morse House on Washington Street. Dating from 1868, it was home to the family whose farmland was developed into what is now South Norwood. The house was deeded to the town by then-owner Charles Bird in 1974, and has been unoccupied since 1999.

The Morse House Restoration Committee is currently working to restore the building and grounds. The committee's vision is to convert the house's first floor into meeting space, and to preserve the second floor as a museum that focuses on Norwood's history. Lending a hand with a spring cleaning of the grounds in 2004 are, from left to right, Mike Nemeskal, Dale Day, Gerard Kelleher, Ed Kniolek, Marie Bernier, and Rick Bernier.

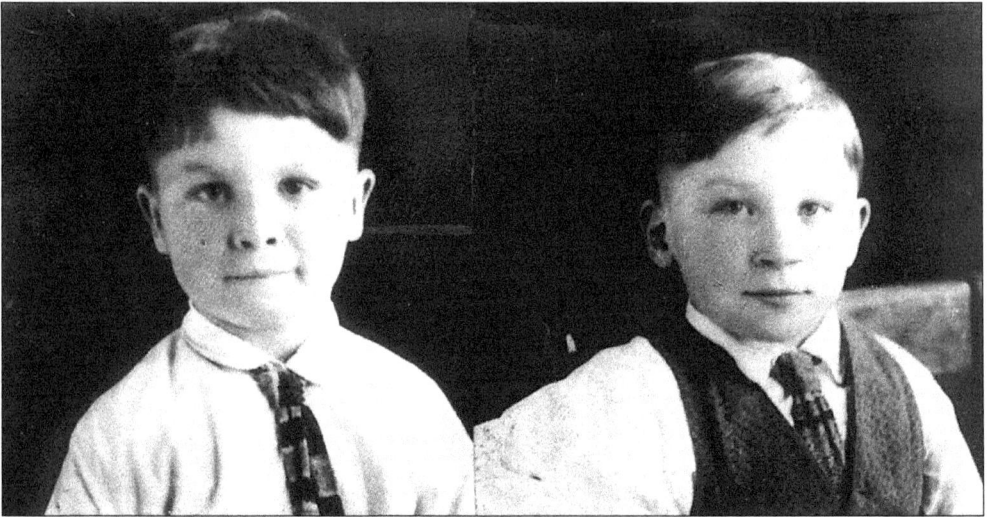

When asked, residents share the sentiment that South Norwood was a wonderful place in which to grow up. And they agree that, for generations, the Balch School has been the heart and soul of the neighborhood. Here, in juxtaposition, are images of the past and the future of this unique community. Above, Fred (left) and Alphonse Babel, the sons of immigrants, were growing up in South Norwood and attending the Balch School in the 1930s when the camera captured them looking bravely toward their future. The two brothers served during World War II, then returned to their old neighborhood. Below, almost 75 years later, during a Balch School field trip, John Nardelli (left) and Alex Cubelli pose behind the tombstone of Congregational church minister Rev. Thomas Balch, after whom their school was named. They, too, face the future with confidence and optimism, having been raised in a neighborhood that still cares.